A General Who Will Fight

A GENERAL WHO WILL FIGHT

The Leadership of Ulysses S. Grant

HARRY S. LAVER

 UNIVERSITY PRESS OF KENTUCKY

Copyright © 2013 by The University Press of Kentucky

Scholarly publisher for the Commonwealth,
serving Bellarmine University, Berea College, Centre College of Kentucky,
Eastern Kentucky University, The Filson Historical Society, Georgetown
College, Kentucky Historical Society, Kentucky State University, Morehead
State University, Murray State University, Northern Kentucky University,
Transylvania University, University of Kentucky, University of Louisville,
and Western Kentucky University.
All rights reserved.

Editorial and Sales Offices: The University Press of Kentucky
663 South Limestone Street, Lexington, Kentucky 40508-4008
www.kentuckypress.com

17 16 15 14 13   5 4 3 2 1

Maps by Dick Gilbreath, University of Kentucky Cartography Lab.

Library of Congress Cataloging-in-Publication Data

Laver, Harry S.
  A general who will fight : the leadership of Ulysses S. Grant / Harry S.
Laver.
      pages cm
  Includes bibliographical references and index.
  ISBN 978-0-8131-3677-6 (hardcover : alk. paper)
  ISBN 978-0-8131-3678-3 (pdf)
  ISBN 978-0-8131-4075-9 (epub)
  1. Grant, Ulysses S. (Ulysses Simpson), 1822-1885—Military leadership.
2. United States—History—Civil War, 1861-1865—Campaigns.
3. Command of troops—Case studies. I. Title.
  E672.L38 2012
  973.7'41092—dc23   2012038941

This book is printed on acid-free paper meeting the requirements of the
American National Standard for Permanence in Paper for Printed Library
Materials.
∞

Manufactured in the United States of America.

Member of the Association of
American University Presses

I have pursued mine enemies, and overtaken them:
　　neither did I turn again till they were consumed.
I have wounded them that they were not able to rise:
　　they are fallen under my feet.
For thou hast girded me with strength unto the battle.
—Psalm 18:37–39

"Well Grant, we've had the devil's own day, haven't we?"
"Yes, lick 'em tomorrow though."
—April 6, 1862

Contents

Maps

Introduction

A Great Force of Will

The Commander must have a great force of will.
—Carl von Clausewitz[1]

Sunday, April 6, 1862, dawned quietly as Ulysses S. Grant sat down at the breakfast table of the Cherry mansion in Savannah, Tennessee. Shuffling through a stack of mail on the table, he leaned forward to take the first sip of coffee when up the Tennessee River valley came the rumbling of artillery fire. With the cup poised at his lips, he paused, listened for a moment, then returned the coffee to the table and announced to his staff, "Gentlemen, the ball is in motion. Let's be off." Making their way out the front door and down stone steps crafted years ago by slaves, he and his staff were soon on board the *Tigress,* whose crew was frantically working to get up a head of steam for the nine-mile trip south to Pittsburg Landing. There, an army of Federal soldiers was camped near a small log Methodist church known locally as the Shiloh Meeting House. Inexplicably, Grant had established his headquarters at distant Savannah on the opposite, eastern side of the river, and, while he spent most of each day with his army, this Sunday morning the Confederates had caught him as unaware as a sleeping sentry.[1]

For the men of Grant's command, the day had begun with the drowsy routine of a Sunday morning. As the first streaks of light ribboned from the eastern sky, nearly forty thousand Union soldiers—and calling them *soldiers* at this point of the war required a bit of imagination—awakened to the clank of pots and pans, the scent of wood smoke and bacon. Mostly farm boys from Iowa, Indiana, Illinois, Ohio, and other midwestern states, this was a green army; some had signed up in January or February, others only a few days ago. The newer regiments had just received their muskets and had yet to master the manual of arms, the precise choreography of loading and firing the weapon. A smattering knew how to march in column and form a line of battle; fewer could maneuver as a unit on the field, even without the unnerving hiss of bullets and shrapnel. The men of Maj. Gen. John McClernand's First Division were the veterans, survivors of the action two months earlier at Forts Henry and Donelson. There, they had caught a glimpse of the mysterious Rebels, delivered their first volley and received the same, and in the process won the first Union victories of the war. But they were the exception; most of the men at Shiloh had not "seen the elephant," and so, despite an abundance of bravado and unearned confidence, they were an army of little training and even less experience, not knowing enough to be wary or watchful. The failure to keep good guard was a shortcoming, not just of these green soldiers and their company captains, but of their senior officers as well, including the army commander, Grant. Now, like most mornings, breakfast campfires drew the men together in small circles, where they contemplated another day of close-order drill and the likely annoyance of a late afternoon rain.

The pop and crackle of desultory musket fire coming from the south was the first indication that something was amiss. Roughly a mile and a half from Shiloh Church, where Fifth Division commander Brig. Gen. William T. Sherman had established his headquarters, Maj. Aaron B. Hardcastle's Third Battalion of Mississippians had attacked. The vanguard of Gen. Albert Sidney Johnston's forty-thousand-strong Army of the Mississippi, Hardcastle's Rebels were driving Union pickets back through forty-acre Fraley field. From across the South, Johnston had gathered this host of Confederates in Corinth, Mississippi, twenty-two miles southwest of Pittsburg Landing. Considered by Jefferson Davis to be the South's best field commander, Johnston had set his army in motion three days earlier with the objective of striking a fatal blow to Grant's invaders before Don Carlos Buell's Army of the Ohio, moving south from Nashville, could reinforce. Brushing aside the concerns of Gen. P. G. T. Beauregard, the

Louisiana Creole known as the "Napoléon in Gray," that the Federals would be "entrenched to the eyes," Johnston swore "to fight them if they were a million." To the Yankee farm boys who now stood in the path of this mounting Confederate tide, the Rebels looked as if *they* were a million as they routed the disorganized Federals across a three-mile-wide maze of twisting roads, wooded thickets, cotton fields, and deep, vine-choked ravines. For Sherman and his men, and in fact for all of Grant's army, surprise, confusion, and inexperience exacerbated the disorientating smoke and thunder of battle.[2]

When around nine o'clock Grant disembarked from the *Tigress* at Pittsburg Landing, he found along the riverbank a roiling mass of men who had fled the fighting, panicked horses straining in their harnesses, and officers shouting with equal futility at both. He ordered more ammunition to the front; then, although still on crutches because of a sprained ankle, he mounted with assistance and made his way forward in search of the fight. On the Union right flank, Sherman and his Fifth Division had put up a stout defense at Shiloh Church before falling back to Jones field, less than a mile from the landing, and that is where Grant found him around ten o'clock. A bloody bandage bound up Sherman's right hand, which throbbed from a wound suffered earlier in the day. It might well have been much worse; seconds before Sherman was hit, an aide, Priv. Thomas Holliday of Illinois, took a bullet to the head, spattering brain and blood across Sherman's face and uniform. Nevertheless, there was fire in his eye, and, seeing that Sherman was doing all he could with what he had, Grant moved to the left to visit his other division commanders. At the center of the battle line, he came on Benjamin Prentiss, the forty-two-year-old Illinois politician who now wore the stars of a brigadier general. Prentiss, whose Sixth Division had absorbed the first Confederate blows in Fraley field, had collected the remnants of his command and spread them out along an old wagon trace that ran perpendicular to the Confederates' line of advance. After assessing the situation, Grant gave orders to Prentiss that were as grim as they were concise: hold your position "at all hazards." Wheeling his horse around, he headed back north, looking to cobble together a last line of defense that would protect Pittsburg Landing and stop the Confederate flood that was swamping the field.[3]

Near the landing, Grant found his chief of staff, Col. Joseph D. Webster, and directed him to anchor the left of the line on the bluff overlooking the Tennessee River, then run it west along the northern lip of the nearly one-hundred-foot-deep Dill Branch ravine. By late afternoon, Webster had aligned ten batteries of artillery, including a massive twenty-four-pounder siege gun intended for operations against Corinth. Herding together stragglers from the riverbank and the remnants of companies that had fought since dawn, officers hurried infantry down the line to support the artillerymen, while the first welcome elements of Buell's army, Jacob Ammen's Ohio brigade, filed into line along the bluff.

Then the Confederates struck. James R. Chalmers's brigade of Mississippians and John K. Jackson's brigade of Alabamians descended into Dill Branch and emerged on its northern rim into a whirlwind of Union rifle and artillery fire. Escaping the storm by falling back into the ravine, Chalmers's men twisted up their courage and again pushed over the top. But again a hail of Union fire drove them back. To their left, Jackson's men fared no better, barely cresting the ravine before tumbling back. As both brigades prepared for yet another assault, word echoed down the line that orders had come to pull back, to break contact with the enemy. General Beauregard, left in command when Albert Sidney Johnston fell mortally wounded around two o'clock, decided they had done enough for one day; the Yankees were beaten and could be finished off in the morning. For Grant, his line had held, but could it stop a Confederate attack that was sure to come the next morning?

Late that evening, as mist and rain settled like a shroud over the battlefield, Sherman picked his way among the scores of sleeping, wounded, and dead in search of Grant, whom he had not seen since their encounter at Jones field earlier in the day. Just above the river landing, Sherman found him crouched under a tree, barely visible in the light of a lantern that struggled feebly against a mix of rain and cigar smoke. At first, neither man spoke, Grant seemingly lost in thought, Sherman taking stock of his commander's mood. "Well, Grant," Sherman finally ventured, "we've had the devil's own day, haven't we?" "Yes," came Grant's studied reply. "Lick 'em tomorrow though."[4]

Given the country's relatively brief history, America has produced a lengthy roster of successful military leaders. Even before the United States had achieved independence, colonial Americans were fighting and winning battles, albeit in a manner that was brutally distinct from the Europeans' practice of formal, limited war. Then as now, innumerable factors determined success on the battlefield—logistics, manpower, alliances, weather, even luck—but most important was leadership. Over the centuries, regardless of time or place, a commander's ability to inspire, to see what his enemy did not see, to make the correct decision at the right moment, or to overcome seemingly insurmountable obstacles has often determined who dictated the terms of surrender.

Manuals and guidebooks on leadership often present an overwhelming collection of qualities deemed necessary for success, including but not limited to integrity, adaptability, cultural and political awareness, charisma, vision, bravery, initiative, judgment, communication, and the list goes on. A few honest leadership theorists have confessed that "the lists suggest that a strategic leader must be, know, and do just about everything." No one, not even Washington, has excelled in every facet of leadership. Consider Robert E. Lee, who demonstrated unparalleled tactical proficiency but failed to define an appropriate strategic vision for the Confederacy; George S. Patton, renowned for his charisma, but also known for stumbling repeatedly in situations that required political sensitivity rather than fiery bravado; and Omar Bradley, whose reserved demeanor was better suited to the professor's lectern than a battlefield command, but who was a pillar of strength and stability for Dwight Eisenhower.[5]

One quality, however, is the common denominator of successful leaders across time and place: *analytical determination*. In his classic *On War*, the Prussian military theorist Carl von Clausewitz identifies among the qualities of military leadership the notion of "a great force of will," which illustrates the fundamental concepts of analytical determination:

> As long as his men full of good courage fight with zeal and spirit, it is seldom necessary for the Chief to show great energy of purpose in the pursuit of his object. But as soon as difficulties arise—and that must always happen when great results are at stake—then things no longer move on of themselves like a well-oiled machine, the machine itself then begins to offer resistance, and to overcome this the Commander must have a great force of will. . . . As the forces in one individual after another become prostrated, and can no longer be excited and supported by an effort of his own will, the whole inertia of the mass gradually rests its weight on the Will of the Commander: by the spark in his breast, by the light of his spirit, the spark of purpose, the light of hope, must be kindled afresh in others: in so far only as he is equal to this, he stands above the masses and continues to be their master; whenever that influence ceases, and his own spirit is no longer strong enough to revive the spirit of all others, the masses drawing him down with them sink into the lower region of animal nature, which shrinks from danger and knows not shame.

Clausewitz alternatively refers to this attribute as "resolution," "energy, firmness, staunchness, strength of mind and character." To these we can add the qualities of self-confidence and mental discipline. Further thought would lengthen the list, but no synonym better captures the essence and spirit of this quality than Clausewitz's original phrase, "a great force of will."[6]

A general may have an effective force structure, unlimited logistical support, outstanding subordinates, and ideal weather and terrain, but soon enough conditions will deteriorate, and events will spiral out of control as the unforeseen and unanticipated rapidly overtake timetables and phase lines. Nevertheless, the effective commander will assess the situation, adapt to the new parameters while keeping the primary objective in sight, and maintain his composure as he presses forward. Put another way, he will have the determination to exercise self-control and control of his command, overcome the voices of self-doubt that rise in moments of crisis, and then make the necessary adjustments to accomplish the mission. Intellectually knowing the proper course is not enough; one must be prepared to act. Recall the 1862 Peninsula campaign, during which Union general George B. McClellan did not press his advantage on the outskirts of Richmond and therefore failed to capture the city, illustrating the momentous consequences of irresolution at a decisive moment. In short, the leader must demonstrate professional competence *and* unshakable resolve—analytical determination.

To be clear, one must not mistake analytical determination for simple stubbornness. The stubborn leader obstinately stays the course, failing to recognize and then respond to changes in the strategic, operational, and tactical environments. The analytical component to determination is often overlooked in favor of aggressiveness, a distinction Clausewitz identified nearly two centuries ago: "The forerunner of resolution *is an act of the mind*." By continually evaluating the environment, making the appropriate adjustments, and maintaining a cool head, analytical determination produces a decision both well conceived and deliberatively made.[7] Maj. Gen. Ambrose E. Burnside's repeated, ill-advised, bloody, and ultimately unsuccessful assaults against Marye's Heights at Fredericksburg reveal a leader unable to distinguish perseverance from pigheadedness. Some have offered such rigidity as an explanation for U. S. Grant's success in the war, that he sacrificed thousands of Union soldiers in frontal assaults whose high costs outweighed minimal gains. He was, the story goes, a butcher, showing little compassion for his men or concern over the roll call of the dead that filled northern newspapers. This argument falters under close scrutiny, and, as we will see, there was much more to Grant's leadership than "Forward charge!"[8]

Historians have long identified Grant's greatest strength as a commander as his determination. They have differed, however, on whether his determination was of the analytical or the stubborn variety. William McFeely, one of Grant's biographers, is a proponent of the stubborn school, arguing that his 1864 Virginia campaign was marked by "inhumanity and inept military strategy that ranks with the worst such episodes in the history of warfare." Recent works by Brooks Simpson, Jean Smith, and Joan Waugh offer more nuanced interpretations that credit Grant with great resolve and a "modern" approach to warmaking. This historiographic debate continues in part because no study of Grant has attempted to explain how one of America's most famous and successful generals developed and then applied his best leadership quality.[9]

What follows is a leadership biography of Ulysses S. Grant that focuses exclusively on how he developed and exercised analytical determination. The art of leadership is a complex human endeavor, denying easy analysis or simple understanding, and it is for that very reason that concentrating on a single factor can bring greater comprehension of the whole. In this instance, an analysis that focuses on the development of Grant's most significant leadership quality can help us better understand his overall style of command and explain his success on the battlefield. In the same manner that one can better comprehend an event as complex as the Civil War by analyzing its individual battles, so too can one more fully appreciate Grant's approach to command by highlighting one, and in this case his best, leadership quality. Given his significance as both a historical figure and a practitioner of military leadership, such a focused study is warranted. Those expecting a comprehensive biography or seeking a grand revision of the general's life and times should look instead to the previously cited traditional biographies. This study is not about the life of Grant; it *is* about the life of his determination and leadership.

While the primary objective of this study is to recount and explain Grant's growth as a leader of determination, an additional intent is to provide aspiring leaders in any field or profession insights on leadership development. Both civilian and soldier have long recognized the value of historical study to the learning and practice of leadership. Case studies of successful entrepreneurs and business innovators are standard fare in the corporate world, while the armed services frequently undertake staff rides to historic battlefields to walk the ground, study the commanders and their decisions, and then evaluate their leadership. Like no other leader in American history, U. S. Grant demonstrated consistent analytical determination in the most challenging of circumstances, and so from him there is much to be learned.[10]

Grant was not born the embodiment of perseverance, nor did he begin his military career armed with unshakable resolve, thereby refuting the notion that great leaders are born, not made, or that leadership skills are innate and cannot be improved on. Instead, Grant developed a will to succeed by applying the advice and guidance of mentors and the hard lessons of experience. An average cadet at West Point, he was a competent junior officer during the Mexican War but fell on hard times in the 1850s. Not until the Civil War and his first significant engagement as a commanding officer did he show evidence that maybe there was something more to this unimposing figure than modest ability and a reputation for drink. Like everyone, he suffered from self-doubt, errors in judgment, and occasional regrets, but a deliberate—and deliberative—will to press forward marked his course to commanding general and victory. He was smart enough to learn from his own mistakes and the mistakes of others, and, when the whirlwind of war threatened to scatter his best-laid plans, he adapted and moved on, always keeping an eye firmly on his strategic objective. Developing analytical determination might not have guaranteed Grant success, but failing to demonstrate such perseverance would almost certainly have condemned him to failure.

During World War II, British field marshal William Slim once told his men, "You all have leadership in you. Develop it by thought, by training, by practice."[11] On the night of April 6, 1862, Grant drew on his training and experience to see that an opportunity existed to reverse the day's setbacks. His decision to hold firm, to seize the initiative the next morning, to "lick 'em tomorrow," revealed in him a strength of will necessary to achieve victory at Shiloh and over the three years of war yet to come.

1

First Lessons

I wish I had more officers like Grant.

—Gen. Zachary Taylor

There was little about the young Hiram Ulysses Grant that hinted he would one day command great armies, win improbable battlefield victories, and become president of the United States. Born to Jesse and Hannah Grant in 1822, he joined a family that was comfortable, if not well-to-do. His father was a tanner who dabbled in local politics, a staunch Democrat, and his mother was a reserved, sober Methodist. There was no sign of an innate military genius in young Grant; in fact, there was no indication of *any* kind of genius. In his memoirs, Grant tells the story of his first venture into horse trading, an experience that reveals more innocent sincerity than native intellect. With the single-mindedness of an eight-year-old boy, he had mercilessly pestered his father for the money to buy a colt from Mr. Ralston, a nearby farmer. When his father finally relented, Ulysses received very specific instructions: first offer $20.00; if he won't take that, offer $22.50; if he won't take that, offer $25.00; but under no circumstances agree to pay any more than that. With money in hand and instructions in mind, Ulysses set off for Ralston's farm and his first experience in dealmaking. Meeting Ralston, he dutifully announced, "Papa says I may offer you twenty dollars for the colt, but if you won't take that, I am to offer twenty-two and a half, and if you won't take that, to give you twenty-five." As Grant went on to observe, "It would not require a Connecticut man to guess the price finally agreed upon." Years later, General Grant would drive a much harder bargain, to the chagrin of more than one Confederate commander.[1]

Jesse Grant, perhaps seeing that his son showed little promise as a businessman, explored other possibilities for Ulysses. He settled on trying to secure an appointment for the boy to the U.S. Military Academy at West Point, New York. In an era when the opportunity to attend college and the money to do so were both in short supply, West Point offered an education at the taxpayers' expense, provided one could obtain an appointment. This the elder Grant was able to pull off by way of his political connections and was pleased when word of admission came from an Ohio senator; the younger Grant, however, did not share his father's enthusiasm. Ulysses, lacking self-confidence and doubting that he could succeed at the academy, wanted no part of a military life: "When [father] read [the letter] he said to me, 'Ulysses, I believe you are going to receive the appointment.' 'What appointment?' I inquired. 'To West Point; I have applied for it.' 'But I won't go,' I said. He said he thought I would, *and I thought so too, if he did.*" Cadet Grant enrolled at West Point in the fall of 1839.[2]

Less than inspired by the path his father had chosen for him, Jesse Grant's son did find modest success at the academy, although more than once the prospect of a "Lieutenant" Grant was less than certain. A few weeks after his fitting in cadet gray, he learned that Congress was considering a bill to abolish West Point, a measure he saw as "an honorable way to obtain a discharge," or, put more bluntly, an easy out for a young man who lacked self-motivation and who had little interest in an army career. He later confessed, "A military life had no charms for me, and I had not the faintest idea of staying in the army even if I should be graduated, which I did not expect." Congress wisely thought better of shuttering the academy, and it remained open, denying Grant an early exit from a life in uniform. In the classroom, he easily conquered math, barely survived two years of French, and voraciously consumed the works of James Fenimore Cooper, Sir Walter Scott, and Washington Irving, among others. Excelling at horsemanship, he held the academy high jump record for more than a quarter century. During his third year, Grant suffered demotion from cadet sergeant to private when he failed to embrace the responsibilities of rank, further confirming the reputation he had established for mediocrity. "The promotion was too much for me," Grant later recalled. Nevertheless, he graduated, placing twenty-first out of thirty-nine cadets in 1843, having shown little of the ability, dash, and military bearing of the Lees, Beauregards, and Johnstons who had recently preceded him. Assigned to the U.S. Army's Fourth Infantry Regiment, itself an indicator of his undistinguished record as the top graduates became engineering or artillery officers, the newly commissioned brevet second lieutenant set out on what should have been an extraordinarily unremarkable military career.[3]

Musket fire north of the Rio Grande River in late April 1846 began the United States' first foreign war. The Mexican-American War sent thousands of Americans off to battle, commanded by the nation's first generation of professionally trained officers. On sun-scorched fields with exotic names like Palo Alto, Chapultepec, and Molino del Rey, Lt. U. S. Grant served under Zachary Taylor and Winfield Scott, learning through experience and observation the practical lessons of leadership. At the same time, the young officer also began to reveal that there might be something more to Jesse and Hannah Grant's son than a good horseman.

One afternoon on the beaches of Corpus Christi, just as General Taylor was setting out on his campaign into northern Mexico, Grant gave a glimpse of the no-nonsense approach to life and leadership that would eventually characterize his command style. Unhappy with his men's efforts to clear underwater obstacles, he dismounted his horse, waded into the surf, and by example demonstrated exactly how he wanted the job done. His waist-deep enthusiasm for what was considered enlisted men's work drew smirks from a few "dandy officers" who poked fun at the lieutenant, but Grant ignored the taunts. Taylor, whose craggy face, straightforward command style, and "Old Rough and Ready" persona suggested he knew something about the hard and dirty work of successful leadership, witnessed the episode. The general recognized what it said about this junior officer: "I wish I had more officers like Grant, who would stand ready to set a personal example when needed."[4]

Similarly, there was much about Taylor that Grant came to admire and even emulate. Taylor, born in Virginia but raised on the frontier, had seen a lifetime's worth of fighting even before the war with Mexico had begun. He seemed to have a nose for battle, first fighting under William Henry Harrison on the Tippecanoe campaign (1811), then joining in the Black Hawk War (1832) and the Second Seminole War (1837). As a commander, Taylor was unmistakably clear in his correspondence and orders. He wanted to see things for himself and cared little for the fineries of military dress; moreover, he was a commander who made the best of a situation and did what he could with what he had. With admiration, Grant recalled that Taylor "was not an officer to trouble the administration much with his demands, but was inclined to do the best he could with the means given him." Years later, President Abraham Lincoln would attribute the same resourcefulness to Grant, but at this moment, as the American army geared up for the push into the prairie and chaparral of northern Mexico, Lieutenant Grant still had those lessons to learn.[5]

Even before President Polk had sent his war message to Congress, Taylor charged his men into battle at Palo Alto on May 8, 1846. Glistening bayonets caught Grant's eye as the Americans deployed in shoulder-high grass, their flintlocks loaded with buck and ball, just out of Mexican artillery range. On order, the infantry surged forward, gaps opening, then closing, as men sidestepped bounding solid shot. Brandishing the bayonet, but relying on the superiority of their artillery, Taylor and his Yankee troops drove the Mexicans off the field at Palo Alto, then south through Resaca de la Palma the following day, and, finally, across the Rio Grande. Despite being outnumbered, the Americans had won two quick victories, but, watching the army's commander as the fighting got under way, Grant came to the realization that, even under favorable circumstances, being in command carried with it tremendous responsibility. "As I looked down that long line of about three thousand armed men, advancing towards a large force also armed," he later recalled, "I thought what a fearful responsibility General Taylor must feel, commanding such a host and so far away from friends." But Taylor, sitting with one leg thrown over his saddle's pommel and squinting from the shade of his broad-brimmed straw hat, never flinched, dead calm amid the chorus of battle. Old Zack did not scare easily, and neither would Grant in his own time.[6]

Taylor pressed both his advantage and the campaign after this initial success, driving farther into the Mexican interior. Grant followed, through Monterrey to Buena Vista, and then, like most of the regulars, joined the second American invasion force under the conspicuous—some might say ostentatious—Gen. Winfield Scott. Scott's leadership style was a study in contrasts compared to that of Taylor. Like Taylor, Scott had fought in the War of 1812, but as a general officer, and the Black Hawk and Second Seminole Wars, after which in 1841 he was named commanding general of the army. Unlike Taylor, he delighted in the trappings of command—the most garnished, if not garish, of uniforms, with a flock of well-accoutred staff officers fluttering in his wake.[7]

From the war's earliest days, Scott had argued that a negotiated settlement of the kind the Polk administration anticipated would require a campaign from the Gulf Coast at Veracruz to the capture of Mexico City itself. Only with the occupation of its capital would the Mexican government accede to American demands, and, while Taylor's northern campaign had been a military success, it had been a political disappointment, failing to gain satisfaction for Polk's demands, proving Scott right. Therefore, on March 9, 1847, Scott set out with ten thousand regulars and volunteers on a march of more than 150 miles into the Mexican heartland, beginning what would become one of history's great military campaigns. Enduring brutal weather, harsh terrain, supply shortages, and the loss of three thousand volunteers whose enlistments expired en route—not to mention Santa Anna and his thirty-thousand-strong Mexican army—Scott and his men lived off the land and fought their way to the gates of the city by early September. Two additional weeks and a series of hard-fought battles won Scott the prize on September 14, concluding an astounding campaign. The Duke of Wellington had been following the war news in Europe and had predicted that Santa Anna and the Mexican terrain would doom the American offensive, but, when word of the victory came, he reversed course and pronounced Scott "the greatest living soldier."[8]

Serving with Scott on this campaign as he had with Taylor, Grant learned additional lessons about command. The march to Mexico City demonstrated the value of reconnaissance, the advantages of enveloping attacks, and the fact that an army could be fed while advancing through a hostile countryside. Of greater significance, Grant saw that Scott's unwavering commitment to press on, despite crippling setbacks, was what in the end decided victory. Scott might have withdrawn to Veracruz more than once, and justifiably so, but, in each instance, after analyzing the obstacles and available options he chose to advance rather than retreat, decisions confirmed by the campaign's successful conclusion. Later assessing the leadership of Taylor and Scott, Grant observed that, "with their opposite characteristics both were great and successful soldiers[,] both were true, patriotic and upright in all their dealings"—and, we might add, good role models for a discerning subordinate. Despite their differences in style, they shared the same determination to succeed. In contrast to the American commanders, Grant also could not help but notice, "The Mexicans fight well for a while, but they do not hold out. They fight and simply quit."[9]

Soon after returning home from the war, Grant obtained leave and traveled to St. Louis, where in August 1848 he married Julia Dent, the sister of a West Point classmate. While he pledged himself to Julia for life, he still belonged to the army. For four years, the couple trooped to postings in Michigan and New York until his regiment received orders for the Pacific Coast, a journey Grant would make on his own, leaving Julia with family in Illinois. In July 1852, the Fourth Infantry sailed from Governor's Island in New York Harbor with Lieutenant Grant serving as regimental quartermaster. After arriving on the Panamanian coast, the regiment made its way across the isthmus by steamboat up the Chagres River to Gorgona, where the men disembarked for the twenty-five-mile march to Panama City and the Pacific. Staying behind to oversee the transport of equipment, Grant discovered that the requisite mules were not available for mustering into the U.S. Army, thanks to an incompetent, if not corrupt, American contractor. Relying on much-improved ingenuity and negotiating skills, Grant parleyed with the locals, bent a few regulations, and eventually recruited sufficient mules to reunite equipment and regiment on the coast. Before he and the goods had departed, however, a wave of cholera struck, afflicting and eventually killing one-third of the soldiers under his command. Sending the healthy on to the coast, Grant stayed behind, carrying on with his normal duties while doing his best to comfort the sick, earning their admiration as a "man of iron" and "the coolest man I ever saw."[10] Grant's steady leadership in Panama demonstrated a maturing confidence and grit; moreover, his resourcefulness and adaptability in handling the mule predicament hinted at a fuller measure of determination than previously shown. These personal victories were unfortunately short-lived as Grant was about to enter his time in purgatory, arguably the most difficult period of his life. In fact, the next seven years would suggest to the undiscriminating eye a distinct *lack* of determination as he struggled to overcome boredom, isolation, and a litany of setbacks that might well have drawn sympathy from Job.

From Panama, Grant continued his journey to the Pacific Northwest, passing through San Francisco, where "at all hours of the day and night . . . the eye was regaled" with dram shops, gambling houses, real estate swindlers, and the waterfront's forest of towering ship masts. His orders took him farther north, first to Fort Vancouver on the Columbia River, and later to Fort Humboldt in northern California. The remoteness of these postings, loneliness and heartache for Julia and their two children, and the hollow solace of drink conspired to leave Grant in a deep melancholy. "He drank far less than other officers," a contractor at Fort Vancouver recalled, but "he had a poor brain for drinking." Life had handed Grant more than he could handle. While the exact circumstances of Grant's departure from the army remain unclear—likely he either was forced out or decided he could not continue such a disheartening existence—the young captain resigned his commission in 1854 and made his way east to a reunion with his family and the hope of a new beginning in the civilian world.[11]

Once back in Illinois, Grant was heartened by Julia and their children, but, beyond the comforts of family, his bad luck gave way to worse. Rather than finding prosperity and peace of mind, he struggled to make ends meet. Financial investments that soured, business ventures that lost money, and a farm that produced mostly heartbreak all pushed Grant toward financial ruin, if not desperation: "If nothing else could be done I would load a cord of wood on a wagon and take it to the city for sale." In 1858, he was struck with "fever and ague," convincing him to give up the plow and try his luck in the real estate market, an experiment that only lengthened his string of failures. Yet, in spite of the relentless beating life was giving him, Grant's spirit and sense of self remained unbroken, revealed in a chance meeting on the streets of St. Louis with an old friend from West Point. Army major and future Confederate general James Longstreet recalled,

> Grant had been unfortunate, and he was really in needy circumstances. . . . The next day . . . I found myself face to face with Grant who, placing in the palm of my hand a five dollar gold piece, insisted that I should take it in payment of a debt of honor over fifteen years old. I peremptorily declined to take it, alleging that he was out of the service and more in need of it than I. "You must take it," said he. . . . Seeing the determination in the man's face, and in order to save him mortification, I took the money, and shaking hands we parted.

Grant's finances may have been in ruin and his prospects for the future bleak, but his integrity and sense of honor remained intact. In fact, the preceding years of failure and frustration revealed in Grant a persistent optimism that life would get better, that his luck would change, that he could be a success, if only the right opportunity came along.[12]

In May 1860, as a divided and apprehensive nation looked ahead to the fall presidential election, Grant's finances remained dismal, putting him at wit's end. With few options and even less money, he reluctantly agreed to clerk in his father's leather goods store in Galena, Illinois.[13] For Grant, having to accept that position was humiliating and demoralizing, not because he saw clerking as beneath him, but because it was an admission of failure—as a soldier, as a businessman, as a farmer, and, by implication, as a man. The sting was particularly sharp as his father had always been, and indeed always would be, a harsh and relentless critic, even as his son rose to the highest level in the military and politics. The fortunes of Jesse Grant's newest employee, however, were about to change.

Deliverance came with the November election, which sent an Illinois lawyer to the White House, a man whose reputed commitment to the abolition of slavery would rend the nation in two. In less than three months, seven states from South Carolina to Texas chose secession over the frustrations of further compromise, irretrievably carrying the nation to civil war. The bark of southern artillery throwing shot at Fort Sumter in the predawn light of April 12, 1861, closed the door to any path but that of war. Meanwhile, across the country in Galena, Illinois, a leather store clerk and former army captain would soon discover that war signaled an end to seven years of poverty, aimlessness, and despondency and opened the door to unimagined opportunities.

2

First Battles

The one who attacks first now will be victorious.

—Ulysses S. Grant

On April 15, 1861, President Lincoln declared the seven seceded states from South Carolina to Texas in rebellion and called for 75,000 volunteers, soon supplemented by another 300,000, to maintain the Union and fulfill his oath to "preserve, protect, and defend the Constitution." Across the North, scores of would-be soldiers answered Lincoln's call to arms in anticipation of patriotic adventure, if not glory, among them former U.S. Army captain Ulysses S. Grant. On June 15, because of his prior service, Grant secured from Illinois governor Richard Yates an appointment as colonel of the Twenty-first Regiment of Volunteers. With a touch of amusement shaded by frustration, Grant remembered that this gathering of "sons of farmers, lawyers, physicians, politicians, merchants, bankers and ministers . . . could be led astray." His first task was to undo the work of their previous commander, who "proved to be fully capable of developing all there was in [the] men of recklessness." At first, the going was anything but easy: "I found it very hard for a few days to bring all the men into anything like subordination; but the great majority favored discipline, and by the application of a little regular army punishment all were reduced to as good discipline as one could ask." Drilled and disciplined at Grant's hand, these sons of Illinois took their first steps to becoming soldiers; nevertheless, as Grant surely suspected, becoming an effective leader would require more than managing the parade ground.[1]

By early July, the Twenty-first was "well up in the company drill" when word came that across the Mississippi River in Missouri Rebels had surrounded another Illinois regiment and Grant's command was to "proceed with all dispatch to their relief." Orders to action had to come at some point, but now, suddenly, the responsibilities of command struck Grant like a thunderbolt—*he* would be the commanding officer on the field, no longer a young lieutenant carried forward by the gravitational pull of larger-than-life warrior-generals like Zachary Taylor and Winfield Scott. Now he had to fill that role, and he doubted he was up to the job. "My sensations," he confessed, "were anything but agreeable. . . . If some one else had been colonel and I had been lieutenant-colonel I do not think I would have felt any trepidation." He was coming to the realization that command was in fact something more than drill and discipline. The fortunes of war, however, determined that it was not yet his time; the encircled regiment found its way home, news that Grant likely received with a mix of relief and disappointment. Circumstances had denied him, at least for the moment, his first test as a combat commander.[2]

If Grant did regret this missed opportunity to try his own worth and that of the regiment, fate and the Confederates gave him another chance two weeks later. This time, the orders were to break up Col. Tom Harris's irregulars, who had taken up camp near Florida, Missouri, a few miles west of Hannibal and the Mississippi River. On July 16, 1861, the regiment made its way across the river and advanced a few miles through a deserted countryside of abandoned farms and homes; no one seemed inclined to welcome the Federals and the war they were likely to bring with them. Amid twilight, the men settled into camp, but for their commander the evening's stillness brought, not peace, but the uncertainty and self-doubt bred by imminent battle.[3]

The advent of day did little to exorcise Grant's fears as the Twenty-first broke camp, formed up in column, and set a course toward Harris's Confederates. Grant's anxiety increased with every step, to the extent that it threatened to cripple his ability to lead: "As we approached the brow of the hill from which it was expected we could see Harris' camp, and possibly find his men ready formed to meet us, my heart kept getting higher and higher until it felt to me as though it was in my throat. I would have given anything then to have been back in Illinois, but I had not the moral courage to halt and consider what to do; I kept right on." Years earlier, in 1845, while Grant was traveling through the Texas wilderness with another lieutenant, they heard the howls of wolves that seemed to be gathering out of sight in the distance, in Grant's mind preparing for an attack. He was more than ready to retreat and retrace their steps, but the other officer "kept on towards the noise, unmoved." Grant "followed in his trail, lacking moral courage to turn back." Now, with unseen Confederates poised to attack, he kept on, again nearly paralyzed by fear. On reaching the crest of the hill, he looked out on the valley and the Confederate camps. He later remembered: "The place where Harris had been encamped a few days before was still there and the marks of a recent encampment were plainly visible, but the troops were gone. My heart resumed its place. It occurred to me at once that Harris had been as much afraid of me as I had been of him. This was a view of the question I had never taken before; but it was one I never forgot afterwards. From that event to the close of the war, I never experienced trepidation upon confronting an enemy, though I always felt more or less anxiety. I never forgot that he had as much reason to fear my forces as I had his. The lesson was valuable."[4]

Valuable indeed. This was a pivotal point in his development as an effective commander, the moment when Grant recognized that the will to succeed stemmed from a deliberate decision to press forward, a conscious choice to confront rather than avoid adversity, and that a commander's resolve was as important as logistics, firepower, or numerical superiority. As he contemplated the enemy's smoldering campfires, he recognized that what separated one commander from another was something simple yet elusive: tenacity. Fear, anxiety, and indecision afflict everyone confronted by a challenge, but an effective leader overcomes these mental obstacles to drive forward. Had he decided to stop the advance, to turn back and retreat from the brow of that hill, he would have failed, both militarily and psychologically, the latter perhaps the most difficult kind of defeat to overcome. The lesson that determination can and must conquer fear and doubt would serve Grant well.

Less than two months later, on September 3, 1861, Confederate general Leonidas Polk crossed the Mississippi River from Missouri to occupy Columbus, Kentucky, a successful military operation that had momentous political consequences, namely, convincing the Kentucky state government to reject secession and openly side with the Union. Grant, now commanding forces in Cairo, Illinois, feared the southerners might press their advantage and seize Paducah, Kentucky, which was strategically important as it commands the confluence of the Tennessee and Ohio Rivers. He telegraphed the department commander, Gen. John C. Fremont, that he "was taking steps to get off that night to be in advance of the enemy in securing that important point": "We started before midnight and arrived early the following morning, anticipating the enemy by probably not over six or eight hours." A month later, little had changed; the Confederates were still in Columbus, and Grant and his command still occupied Paducah, impatiently so, as a letter to his wife, Julia, reveals: "I am very sorry that I have not got a force to go south. . . . There is but very little doubt, no doubt, but that we can hold this place. What I want is to advance." Even though Grant had yet to take his Illinois boys up against the Rebels, Elihu Washburne, the Galena congressman who had become Grant's patron in Washington and would remain so throughout the war, on August 5 secured Grant a promotion to brigadier general. Washburne believed him to be "one of the best officers in the army, [who] is doing wonders in bringing order out of chaos. He is as incorruptible as he is brave." Soon Grant would prove his courage, but, as for being one of the army's best, that would take a little longer.[5]

The opportunity to advance came with the arrival of orders from Fremont directing Grant to take his regiment once more into Missouri, opposite Polk's forces at Columbus, Kentucky. His combined arms force of five infantry regiments, a battery of artillery, and cavalry scouts was to cross the Mississippi River and move against the Confederate outpost at Belmont, a staging camp for enemy operations into the state's interior. A demonstration is all Fremont had in mind, looking for Grant to keep southern eyes cast toward the Mississippi and away from operations farther west. Grant well understood his commander's intent, acknowledging, "I had no orders which contemplated an attack by the National troops, nor did I intend anything of the kind when I started out from Cairo." Nevertheless, he would fail to convert his chief's intentions into action, allowing the emotions of the campaign to affect his decisionmaking. Once the march began, he recalled, "I did not see how I could maintain discipline, or retain the confidence of my command, if we should return to Cairo without an effort to do something." True enough perhaps, but his orders were clear, and this would not be the last time the new general would surrender his command responsibilities to the caprice of circumstance.[6]

The rising sun on November 7, 1861, revealed Grant's men balancing their way down planks as they disembarked from naval transports, landing on the Mississippi's western bank about three miles north of Belmont, out of the Confederates' line of sight. By 8:00 A.M., the Federals were making their way toward the southerners' camp when on the far side of a thick stand of trees shots rang out. The skirmishers had made contact, and Grant's long-anticipated first battle was on. The Confederates soon began to fall back, motivated by inexperience, poor leadership, and Federal rifle and artillery fire. Passing through their own camps, they hardly slowed before reaching the muddy wash of the Mississippi. With the enemy routed and the frustrations of earlier near battles forgotten, Grant could finally celebrate his first fight with the enemy. But, if the truth be told, this was a soldiers' fight, with the men following the battle's ebb and flow rather than directions from the army's commander. The troops had for the most part fought this battle on their own as Grant had issued few orders and, with a minimal staff, knew little of what was happening beyond the limits of eye and ear. He cheered, he encouraged, he berated, but he did little to keep his hands on the fight. Yet the day had been won, or so it seemed.[7]

In truth, Grant had allowed events and the men themselves to take over the battle rather than exercise his authority and responsibility as commander to control the fight, and the result was a near disaster. "The moment the camp was reached," Grant admitted, "our men laid down their arms and commenced rummaging the tents to pick up trophies. Some of the higher officers were little better than the privates. They galloped about from one cluster of men to another and at every halt delivered a short eulogy upon the Union cause and the achievements of the command." Grant's criticism of the officer corps is justified, but one must also ask where *he* was while his army disintegrated into a plundering mob. He had lost control of his men and was about to learn a hard lesson about command.[8]

As the Federals pillaged tents and knapsacks for food and meager booty, along the banks of the river Confederate officers were pulling their men into line of battle. In minutes, the southerners swept back through the camps, driving bewildered and confused Yankees before them. Grant saw flashes of panic in his men's eyes as he struggled to regain control, shouting "that we had cut our way in and could cut our way out just as well." Following his lead, the bluecoats began to form up and regained a measure of composure before fighting their way back to the riverboats, Confederate shot and shell peppering the air as they made their escape. Grant oversaw the retreat and was the last Union man to board, gingerly guiding his horse up the gangplank and onto the ship's deck, denying the southerners a full measure of revenge.[9]

The next day, having returned to his headquarters in Cairo, Grant was ebullient. Writing to his fellow brigadier general Charles F. Smith, he exulted in his conquest: "We drove the Rebels completely from Belmont, burned their tents, and carried off their artillery, for want of horses to draw them, we had to leave all but two pieces on the field. The victory was complete." To Seth Williams, the assistant adjutant general in Washington, he wrote that "the object of the expedition was to prevent the enemy from sending out reinforcements," and his men had accomplished that mission. The day was everything Grant could have hoped for.[10]

Not everyone, however, was so quick to declare victory. One Illinois soldier thought little of his commander's performance: "Grant got whipped at Belmont, and that scared him so that he counter-manded all our orders and took all the troops back to their old sta-tions by forced marches." More serious condemnation came from Col. W. H. L. Wallace, who led the Eleventh Illinois regiment and as a division commander would fall to a mortal wound at Shiloh five months later. In a candid assessment of the battle, Wallace wrote to his wife, "[Grant] had not the courage to refuse to fight. The advantages were all against him and any permanent or substantial good an utter impossibility under the circumstances. I see that he and his friends call it a victory, but if such be victory, God save us from defeat."[11]

So what are we to make of Grant's Belmont excursion, his first meaningful test as a combat commander? His own assessment not-withstanding, he committed a number of significant mistakes, some of them serious enough to have threatened the survival of his com-mand. His lack of situational awareness and poor command and con-trol invited disaster, including higher casualties, if not capture and defeat. In the early hours of the fight, he failed to anticipate what the Confederates might do next, and not until his army came under attack while in the midst of pillaging did he seem to realize that his opponent still had a say in the battle's outcome. Moreover, despite fully understanding his commander's intent to carry out only a dem-onstration, he interpreted Fremont's orders to suit his own objective of getting into a fight, thereby failing to recognize or, even worse, respect the broader strategic objectives.

Grant erred more than once at Belmont, and his mistakes were not inconsequential, but those failures must be balanced against his inexperience and signs of a maturing leadership ability. He had after all drawn southern attention away from action farther west, which was the primary objective for the expedition, and in the process gained experience for his troops that would "be of incalculable ben-efit to us in the future." Equally so, he gained experience and faith in himself, now having a real battle under his belt, which "has given me a confidence in the Officers and men of this command, that will enable me to lead them in any future engagement without fear of the result." He also showed great physical courage, losing one horse to Confederate fire, and an ability to inspire as he rode among the men. John McClernand, the prickly Illinois politician-turned-officer who would torment Grant for much of the war, praised him and his effect on the men, who were "stimulated by your presence and inspired by your example." Most important in assessing Grant is that, at the critical moment when the battle's outcome hung in the balance, when panic threatened the very survival of his army, he revealed a force of will strong enough to drive his men through the rejuvenated Confederates and back to their riverboat escape. And, while he might have stretched his orders, his doing so demonstrated an aggressiveness rare among Union commanders, then or later. Indeed, Confederate general Leonidas Polk took the measure of Grant after the dust settled at Belmont: "He is undoubtedly a man of much force." At this point of the war, Grant showed more stubbornness than analytical determination by advancing without first assessing the situation, but he had learned from his encounter with the Confederates, just as he had learned from the mere threat of a fight a few months earlier. Such lessons would prove invaluable in the coming months.[12]

January 1862 found Grant and his command again encamped at Cairo, Illinois, restless and anxious to strike south. While the fight at Belmont had not been a "complete victory," as Grant had characterized it, the experience had done little to dampen the aggressiveness he had shown prior to the engagement. Looking to establish the initiative, he traveled to St. Louis to propose a campaign against the Rebel stronghold at Fort Henry to Gen. Henry W. Halleck, his immediate superior and the commander of the Department of Missouri. Located on the east bank of the Tennessee River just south of the Kentucky-Tennessee border, Fort Henry was one of two key river fortifications in Confederate general Albert Sidney Johnston's defensive line, which ran from Columbus, Kentucky, in the west to the Cumberland Gap in eastern Tennessee. The fort's artillery precluded any thought of a Union naval thrust along the river, a conduit through Tennessee into northern Mississippi and Alabama. Just ten miles to the east on the Cumberland River was the second of the river strongholds, Fort Donelson, designed to stop the Federals from moving south to Nashville.

At least initially, Halleck was less than impressed with his subordinate's attempt at strategic planning, and, given Halleck's record and reputation, this might have been expected. An 1837 graduate of West Point, Halleck was the army's resident intellectual, having taught classes at the academy while still a cadet, later lecturing on fortification theory and translating a work by the French military theorist Henri Jomini. At the war's start, Winfield Scott had considered Halleck one of the army's smartest officers, an assessment with which Halleck fully concurred, so it does not surprise that Halleck viewed Grant as an amateur—and one with a reputation for hard drinking at that—attempting to dictate strategy to the professional. Not unexpectedly then, Grant received a chilly reception in St. Louis: "I had not uttered many sentences before I was cut short as if my plan was preposterous." "Old Brains" Halleck then outlined a campaign that better fit his methodical—some might say plodding—temperament, a demonstration in the direction of Nashville: "Make a great fuss about moving *all* your forces toward Nashville. . . . Having accomplished this, you will slowly retire to your former positions, but, if possible keep up the idea of a general advance. Be very careful however to avoid a battle. We are not ready for that." Make a fuss, retreat, avoid battle; one can only imagine Grant's frustration, a sentiment not unlike that which was beginning to take hold of President Lincoln back in Washington. His desire for something, *anything,* to happen would soon produce his General Order No. 1, instructing all military commanders to advance on or before February 22, the upcoming anniversary of Washington's birthday. In truth not anticipating that all would comply, the president hoped to see at least some movement forward.[13]

Unlike Lincoln, Grant was in direct command of troops and therefore could better press the matter. Unwilling to give up on his Fort Henry idea, he secured the support of the U.S. Navy in the person of Flag Officer Henry Foote, a crusty forty-year veteran of the sea service and the commander of the Mississippi River Squadron, a man who shared Grant's eagerness to do *something*. Grant and Foote entered into a cooperative and pragmatic relationship, a practice Grant repeated with his naval counterparts throughout the war, showing an ability that enhanced the effectiveness of his campaigns and today serves as a model for conducting joint operations at the senior command level. In this instance, Foote threw his weight behind the young general's plan, giving it a mark of legitimacy sufficient to win over the reluctant Halleck. On February 2, 1862, Grant's soldiers and Foote's sailors steamed out of Cairo on riverboats, heading south on the Tennessee River, bound for Fort Henry and the first significant Union invasion of the Confederacy.[14]

"All the troops will be up by noon tomorrow," Grant wrote to wife, Julia, on February 4 as the flotilla crossed from Kentucky into Tennessee and drew near Fort Henry. He radiated a self-confidence that had undertones of brashness, signs of a commander with just enough experience to be overly sure of himself: "The enemy are well fortified and have a strong force. I do not want to boast but I have a confident feeling of success. You will soon hear if my presentiment is realized." Two days later, Grant received word that the Confederates were moving to reinforce Fort Henry, which we now know was incorrect; nevertheless, he believed that the enemy was strengthening, so he had to make a decision: attack immediately or withdraw. He did not hesitate: "The fort should be carried today." The infantry soon disembarked from transports, while Foote's river fleet turned its sights on Fort Henry. The naval gunners did their work effectively and efficiently, forcing the fort's garrison to surrender after a short bombardment and before Grant's soldiers could work their way through the muck and mud of the riverbank. A telegram from Grant announced the victory to Halleck: "Fort Henry is ours. . . . I shall take and destroy Fort Donaldson [*sic*] on the eighth and return to Fort Henry." Grant may have been tempted to pause and enjoy his success, perhaps gloat a little in Halleck's direction. After all, he and Foote had pulled off the first significant Union victory of the war, a success achieved in great measure by his initiative, but his inclination was to keep moving. He was determined to push on as he made clear in a note to his sister: "I intend to keep the ball moving as lively as possible." And keep it moving he did. Seven months and two and a half battles into the war, his approach to leading and fighting was beginning to take form.[15]

The day after the anticlimactic occupation of Fort Henry, and as rains began to cascade down, Grant issued orders for his men "to be prepared at any hour in the morning for a move, with two days rations in their haversacks." Taking a few days to organize for the march, prepare his lines of communication, and give Foote time to shift his gunboats to Fort Donelson on the Cumberland River would have been a reasonable plan, but even at this early stage of the war it was not in Grant's nature to dawdle: "I was very impatient to get to Fort Donelson because I knew the importance of the place to the enemy. . . . I felt that 15,000 men on the 8th would be more effective than 50,000 a month later." Keep moving, keep pushing, keep pressing—Grant was loathe to surrender the initiative. His ambition to maintain the campaign's momentum, however, did not overwhelm good judgment. He ordered the collection of the Confederates' abandoned artillery, wagons, and equipment, and, on February 8, he reluctantly postponed the advance because heavy rains and high water "prevented acting offensively as I should like to do."[16]

In a few days, skies had cleared sufficiently for Grant's command, recently named the Army of the Tennessee, to slog through ten or so miles of Tennessee mud to Fort Donelson. There, suffering from freezing temperatures, they set up a perimeter trapping the fort's defenders against the Cumberland River. Compared to the easily conquered Fort Henry, Donelson was better located, engineered, and armed and thus more dangerous, as Foote's gunboats discovered on February 14 when they engaged its batteries in the hopes of scoring a second victory in less than ten days. This time, the Rebels gave as good as they got. Solid shot and shell pummeled the Union fleet, splintering hulls, and slicking the decks with sailors' blood. Foote himself went down wounded when shot ripped through the wheelhouse of his ship, the *St. Louis*. Realizing that another easy victory was not in the offing, the fleet backtracked out of Donelson's reach. This time, Grant's foot soldiers would have to finish the job.

Foote's wounds were not life threatening, so the following day Grant rode out to the *St. Louis* to confer. He had been there but a short time when a frantic courier arrived with news that the Confederates had attacked the Union line and a desperate fight was under way. Grant raced back to camp and, as at Belmont three months earlier, there found that confusion and chaos were overwhelming his army. In a move that surprised everyone in blue, including General Grant, the southerners had struck the Union right flank in an attempt to escape to the south and join Albert Sidney Johnston's forces at Nashville. Listening to the panicked reports of Gen. John McClernand and Gen. Lew Wallace, Grant paused a moment to assess the situation. Then with understated determination he issued his orders: "Gentlemen, the position on the right must be retaken." Sensing that the southerners were as disorganized as his own army, he understood that the next few moments could well decide the battle's outcome and that the commander who seized the initiative had the best chance of victory. After requesting assistance from Foote, he ordered his men to advance, despite their confusion: "The one who attacks first now will be victorious and the enemy will have to be in a hurry if he gets ahead of me."[17]

The Yankees surged forward, got ahead of the Confederates, and took advantage of the Rebels' own confusion to drive them back into Fort Donelson. The following day, it fell to Confederate general Simon Bolivar Buckner, a friend of Grant's who had fought with him in Mexico, to request terms of surrender. This drew a terse response from Grant, who was not inclined to let old friendships get in the way of fighting a war. Moreover, when Buckner's initial note arrived in the Union camp, Grant sought the opinion of one of his division commanders, Charles F. Smith, who was no more inclined to negotiate than Grant: "No terms to the damned Rebels!" Grant then sat down and penned a brief reply to Buckner: "No terms except an unconditional and immediate surrender can be accepted. I propose to move immediately upon your works." With Grant holding all the cards, Buckner had little choice but to "accept the ungenerous and unchivalrous terms which you propose." Unchivalrous perhaps, but Grant had achieved another victory, fairly won. Similar to his concise message ten days earlier announcing the surrender of Fort Henry, the telegraph Grant sent Halleck on February 16 read, "We have taken Fort Donelson." On February 17, as Abraham Lincoln signed Grant's promotion to major general, he opined to Secretary of War Edwin Stanton, "If the Southerners think that man for man they are better than our Illinois men, or Western men generally, they will discover themselves in a grievous mistake." "Unconditional Surrender" Grant was making a name for himself with the people who mattered, and he was doing so by winning battles.[18]

Grant had orchestrated two significant Union victories in the short span of ten days; nevertheless, the army commander had again made a number of mistakes. As at Belmont, he had failed to anticipate what the Confederates might do, instead thinking only about what *he* was going to do. Once his men had encircled Fort Donelson, his focus was fixed on his next move, without considering that the Confederates likely had plans of their own. His tunnel vision also affected his division commanders, Wallace and McClernand, who without guidance from their commander were paralyzed when the southerners decided to follow their own script. Grant should not be faulted for being caught away from the field when the Confederates struck as he had a legitimate need to confer with the wounded Foote; however, he did err in failing to foresee that a breakout attempt was possible, if not likely, and thus prepare his subordinates for such a contingency.

That being said, Grant continued to grow as a leader, showing the determination to overcome both man-made and natural obstacles, including those born of self-doubt, inherent in any undertaking of consequence. General Wallace, writing after the war, identified the significance of the Battle of Fort Donelson and what it revealed about his commander's developing leadership: "In every great man's career there is a crisis exactly similar to that which now overtook General Grant, and it cannot be better described than as a crucial test of his nature. . . . He saw with painful distinctness the effect of the disaster to his right wing. . . . But in an instant these signs of disappointment or hesitation . . . cleared away." At that moment, Grant took stock of the situation and issued the orders to close the right flank, and, while in retrospect this course hardly seems to have required great ingenuity, the crisis had immobilized both Wallace and McClernand. When the battle hung in the balance, Grant chose to attack, putting into practice the lesson that he had learned the previous summer in Missouri. This time, unlike at Belmont, he was in command of himself, his men, and the battle, assessing events, adapting as necessary, making appropriate decisions, and moving with force and determination. His leadership style was understated, which was his nature; there were no histrionics, no appeals to God, country, or honor. "In battle, as in camp," Wallace observed, "he went about quietly, speaking in a conversational tone; yet he appeared to see everything that went on, and was always intent on business." And that business was winning battles.[19]

During this campaign, Grant had the good fortune to count among his division commanders Brig. Gen. Charles F. Smith. Smith, older and more experienced than most officers in the army at the time, had been the commandant at West Point twenty years earlier when Grant was a cadet and had become one of the army's most respected officers. Lew Wallace described him as "a person of superb physique, very tall, perfectly proportioned, straight, square-shouldered, ruddy-faced, with eyes of perfect blue, and long snow-white mustaches. He seemed to know the army regulations by heart." The fortunes of war had created an awkward situation for both men as Grant was now the commanding officer, but as the 1862 campaign progressed Grant sought advice and guidance from Smith, whom he saw as the equal of Winfield Scott and "much fitter . . . for command of all the forces in the . . . district than I was." Nevertheless, the two enjoyed a rewarding relationship, with Grant being overly deferential while Smith acted the loyal subordinate. "Grant is a very modest person," Smith wrote. "From old awe of me—he was one of my pupils from 1838 to 1842 (I think)—he dislikes to give me an order and says I ought to be in his place." When a question arose of Smith's loyalty to the Union, Grant sprang to his defense, telling Illinois congressman Elihu Washburne, "There is no doubt of his loyalty and efficiency. We Cant [*sic*] spare him now."[20]

Separated by age and appearance, the two men were still of like minds on how to carry out war. Smith believed that a leader must always be prepared for the fight. "Battle," he wrote, "is the ultimate to which the whole life's labor of an officer should be directed. He . . . must always be getting ready for it exactly as if he knew the hour of the day it is to break upon him. And then, whether it come late or early, he must be willing to fight—he *must* fight." Later, when Grant described his philosophy of war, Smith's influence was apparent: "The art of war is simple enough. Find out where your enemy is. Get at him as soon as you can. Strike him as hard as you can, and keep moving." Smith would die from an infected leg wound before the end of April 1862, and, while Grant would miss his steadying influence, the young general recognized the value of his mentoring, and his lessons were not forgotten.[21]

The Yankees' capture of Forts Henry and Donelson did more than up the Federals' score by two; it broke the Confederates' grip on two waterways that flowed through the heart of Dixie, two rivers that could now carry the enemy's invading legions deeper into Tennessee and Mississippi. Col. Cadwallader C. Washburn, a member of Grant's staff, concluded, "The capture of [Fort Donelson] was the capture virtually of Nashville, and settles the rebellion throughout the valley of the Mississippi." Although Washburn's assessment rings more of excessive optimism than measured foresight, Grant had certainly turned his thoughts in that direction. After dictating surrender terms to the Fort Donelson Confederates on February 16, he telegraphed Halleck that he intended to move next against Clarksville, Tennessee, about halfway to Nashville, but first Foote's gunboats had to refit from their duel with Donelson. Three days later, Halleck learned that the southerners had pulled out of Clarksville on their own and that Grant expected to occupy the town on the twenty-first; moreover, still looking to keep the ball moving, Grant wanted to push straight on to Tennessee's capital city: "It is my impression that by following up our success Nashville would be an easy conquest." Commodore Foote agreed, writing, "General Grant and I believe we can take Nashville."[22]

For Halleck, this was too much, too fast. Believing his two subordinates "impatient," he ordered Grant to permit the gunboats to target only bridges and rail lines in the vicinity of Clarksville, then have them return to Cairo, where the expedition had started two weeks earlier. In a note to Grant, Foote confirmed that the campaign was racing past the cautious-minded Halleck and that the commanding general was indeed putting on the brakes, directing "that everything remains in 'Statu quo' [*sic*] or as they now are." Grant, looking "to make a new subject soon," began chafing under Halleck's leaden hand and, in another sign of his growing self-confidence, imagined the freedoms of an independent command. "I have done a good job at Forts Henry and Donelson," he wrote to Julia on March 1, "but I am being so much crippled in my resources that I very much fear that I shall not be able to advance so rapidly as I would like. . . . I do hope that I will be placed in a seperate [*sic*] Department so as to be more independent." Grant's wish to press on came, not from blind ambition, but from a belief that momentum was on his side, that the successes at Henry and Donelson had thrown the Confederates off balance and likely demoralized their troops. "'Secesh,'" he speculated, "is now about on its last legs in Tennessee." Equally important, if not more so, the army commander was conscious of the human cost of a hard campaign. Here, in February 1862, Grant outlined an approach to war that would characterize his command for the next three years: "I want to push on as rapidly as possible to save hard fighting. These terrible battles are very good things to read about for persons who lose no friends but I am decidedly in favor of having as little of it as possible. The way to avoid it is to push forward as vigorously as possible." And so he would try to do.[23]

Despite Halleck's hesitations, the Army of the Tennessee did push on to occupy Nashville on February 23. This string of victories, crowned by the capture of the first Confederate state capital, ironically brought a demoralizing setback for Grant, and it originated, not from the enemy, but from his commander. Rumors, exaggerated as they were, about Grant having returned to the bottle cast a shadow over Henry and Donelson, especially among those inclined to professional jealousy and already prejudiced by Grant's reputation for drink. Never fond of overachieving subordinates, Halleck gave more ear to the whisperings than he should have, but more worrisome to the department commander was Grant's apparent refusal to maintain communications while in the field. When word came that Grant had traveled to Nashville without orders, Halleck's patience ran out. He complained to General-in-Chief George McClellan in Washington, "I can get no returns, no reports, no information of any kind from him. Satisfied with his victory, he sits down and enjoys it without any regard to the future." With McClellan's nod of approval, Halleck, who could not have been more wrong, relieved Grant on March 4 and gave command of the army to the ailing Charles Smith.[24]

Grant, dumbfounded by Halleck's recriminations and his removal from command, struggled to understand why the sky had suddenly fallen, especially in light of the success he and his men had achieved against the Rebels. He knew, as evidence now confirms, that he had not slipped into the bottle, that he had responded to all Halleck's telegrams, and that he had conducted himself in a most professional manner. What neither Grant nor Halleck knew was that a telegraph operator with southern sympathies had waylaid communications between the two officers, but, rather than give his winning general the benefit of the doubt, Halleck listened to the rumors that confirmed his own preconceptions and prejudices. Grant dutifully turned command over to Smith as the army began making its way south on the Tennessee River. Despite the unjust and public upbraiding he had received at the hands of Halleck, he assisted Smith as best he could in pursuit of the Confederates, assuring him, "I will remain at Fort Henry and throw forward all the troops that can be provided with transportation."[25]

Redemption came when Halleck reinstated Grant on March 14, primarily because Lincoln had taken an interest in the matter, unwilling to lose a fighting general who had actually won a battle, a commodity not to be cast aside lightly. Grant had survived his first engagement in army politics, but it would not be his last, and future battles in that theater would test his determination as much as the Confederates. For now, however, he once again set his sights south, looking to press his advantage against the retreating and demoralized army of Sidney Johnston.[26]

By mid-March 1862, Grant's men, working in cooperation with Foote's naval forces, had shattered the Confederates' hopes of holding the Kentucky-Tennessee line, captured two forts and one state capital, and done so at a tolerable cost. Neither the campaign nor its generals had been perfect, but the Union commanders had learned some important lessons about their men and themselves. Grant had failed to demonstrate consistent command and control over his army, especially at Belmont, but also at Fort Donelson, where he neglected to prepare his subordinates for the unexpected, namely, a Confederate attack. In each engagement, he also seemed to discount or ignore the enemy's ability to act on his own accord, resulting in repeated failures to anticipate Confederate attacks.

Grant did, nevertheless, show that he had learned something from these first battles, including a belief in himself and an increased confidence in his ability to command. At Belmont, he saw the price of giving free rein to a battle and thereafter worked to keep a tighter grip on his army at Donelson. Most important, he began to show signs of a developing analytical determination. His commitment to victory revealed itself during the chaos at Belmont and Donelson as well as between engagements with his desire to press on from Henry to Donelson, from Donelson to Clarksville, and, ultimately, in the pursuit of Johnston's army. If Halleck remained unconvinced, Grant's men were starting to see that there was something of substance in their rumpled, unimposing general. At least eleven officers, including John McClernand, the most senior and least likely to offer professional compliments, voiced their support in a common letter, telling Grant, "Under your lead the flag of the Union has been carried from the interior further towards the seaboard than by any other hands. You have slain more of the enemy, taken more prisoners and trophies, lost more men in battle and regained more territory to the Union than any other leader." Others in Grant's command gave him a ceremonial sword in honor of his "brilliant success" and their "confidence in your ability as a commander." His men had been bloodied, he had learned something about command and about himself, and now he looked ahead to the next campaign, toward Corinth, Mississippi, where he expected to destroy Johnston's Confederates.[27]

3

Shiloh

Lick 'em tomorrow.
— Ulysses S. Grant

Just days before his ill-advised relief of General Grant on March 4, 1862, Henry Halleck had outlined strategic objectives for the coming campaign, including the destruction of a railroad bridge near Eastport, Mississippi, followed by strikes against the rail centers of Corinth and Jackson. Now back in command and happy to have rejoined his army, Grant was intent on going "with the expedition to Corinth in person," but chastened after his run-in with Halleck he vowed to "take no risk . . . under the instructions I now have." While he planned to exercise greater caution with his superiors, his commitment to keeping pressure on the Confederates remained firm. Gen. Charles F. Smith had taken the army to Pittsburg Landing, about twenty miles northeast of Corinth on the Tennessee River, where Iowa and Indiana farm boys drilled in preparation for the anticipated move against the Rebels. Confirmed now in his thinking that relentless pursuit of the enemy, never giving them an opportunity to regroup or seize the initiative, was the best way to gain the most at the least cost, Grant notified Smith that he intended to attack Corinth sooner rather than later. "I am clearly of the opinion," he told his former West Point commandant, "that the enemy are gathering strength at Corinth quite as rapidly as we are here, and the sooner we attack, the easier will be the task of taking the place."[1]

The Confederates, under Albert Sidney Johnston, were indeed gathering at Corinth, but the Federals had reinforcements on the march as well. Halleck had ordered Don Carlos Buell's Army of the Ohio to advance southwest from Nashville, link up with Grant, and with the combined armies strike a deathblow at Corinth. As March gave way to April, Grant's Yankees at Pittsburg Landing continued to train while awaiting Buell's arrival. Word among the locals hinted that the Confederates might be coiling for a preemptive attack of their own from the west, and, although Grant put his division commanders on alert, he remained confident that he held the initiative and that two months of retreat had sapped the southerners' offensive spirit. "I have scarsely [sic] the faintest idea of an attack, (general one,) being made upon us but will be prepared should such a thing take place," he telegraphed Halleck on April 5. The following morning, Johnston's men, who were supposedly too defeated and demoralized to contemplate anything but a half-hearted defense of Corinth, came roaring out of the dawn mist in Fraley's field just south of Shiloh Church. They caught the bluecoats by surprise and drove them north, interrupting Grant's morning coffee nine miles away in Savannah.[2]

After what must have seemed an interminable ride to Pittsburg Landing on the *Tigress*, Grant made his way up to the battlefield on horseback. Riding amid the chaos as he sought out his division commanders, he showed no "evidence of excitement or trepidation" even when a spent bullet struck and bent his scabbard. He sent word to Buell's men, who were near Savannah, to press forward with all possible speed: "The appearance of fresh troops on the field now would have a powerful effect both by inspiring our men and disheartining [sic] the enemy." After directing Benjamin Prentiss to hold the center of the line "at all hazards," he returned to the landing, where he supervised frantic efforts to cobble together a defensive line of sufficient strength to hold against the last exhausted wave of Confederates. As dusk cooled the fighting into desultory musket fire, Grant sat stoically on his horse, watching the southern tide recede. A beleaguered Federal soldier overheard the general mutter, "Not beaten yet by a damn sight." When pressed by a newspaper reporter to comment on the desperate situation, Grant replied, "They can't break our lines

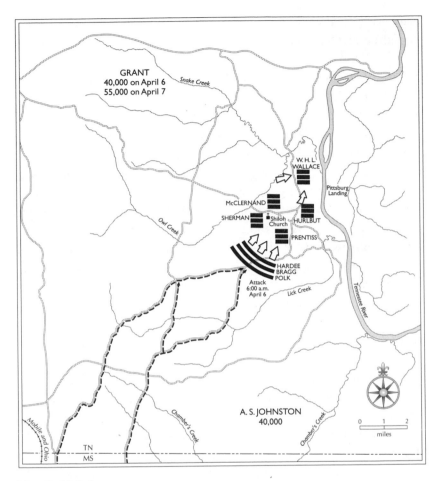

Map 1. Shiloh

tonight—it is too late. Tomorrow we shall attack them with fresh troops and drive them, of course."[3]

Few shared his optimism. Col. James B. McPherson, a promising officer destined to command the Seventeenth Corps at Vicksburg and later the Army of the Tennessee, raised the issue of withdrawal: "General Grant, under this condition of affairs, what do you propose to do, sir? Shall I make preparations for retreat?" Again Grant brushed aside any thought of withdrawal: "No. I propose to attack at daylight and whip them." Despite the day's brutal fighting that seemingly gave the southerners the upper hand, Grant recognized that the enemy was likely spent and that Union reinforcements were at hand. He was confident in himself and in his men, and this he conveyed to Sherman with the assurance that they would "Lick 'em tomorrow."[4]

Sherman was undoubtedly surprised with Grant's reply. The Union army had suffered terrible casualties, had lost its cohesion, energy, and spirit, and was teetering on the edge of annihilation. True, even as the two generals conferred on the bluffs overlooking the landing, the brigades of Buell's reinforcing legions were making their way across the river and into line, but a concerted Confederate attack might well drive the Federals into the Tennessee River. The fate of the northern armies, and indeed the Union war effort in Tennessee, rested on Grant, and, despite advice from his subordinates throughout the evening to retreat, he chose to stay. Regardless of the day's setbacks, his experience told him that the next day could bring victory, but only if he had the determination to stick it out and fight.

Tough talk is easy, but Grant was prepared to follow through. He notified Buell that the army would attack at first light with cavalry scouts preceding infantry and artillery; to Sherman he sent word "to be ready to assume the offensive in the morning." He explained his reasoning in a report submitted two days later, on April 9: "[I felt] that a great moral advantage would be gained by becoming the attacking party, and advance was ordered as soon as day dawned." The rising sun of April 7 found the night rains gone and the Federals in motion. Grant's battle-worn soldiers and Buell's fresh reinforcements hit the exhausted southerners hard, but the Rebels did not give way easily. Brutal fighting raged again through the Hornets' Nest and Duncan Field and around Water Oaks Pond, with charge met by countercharge. By midafternoon, P. G. T. Beauregard's Confederates had held firm longer than even the most sanguine might have hoped, but in truth they were finished. Grant, sensing that the southerners "were ready to break and only wanted a little encouragement from us to go quickly," pulled into a line whatever men he could gather and led them forward himself, "with loud cheers and with a run." Beauregard realized that while the army's spirit was willing its flesh had been weakened by a two-day bloodletting; he reluctantly ordered a withdrawal to Corinth, forced to retreat before the flood of blue-clad Yankees. With his own army wounded and exhausted, Grant declined to pursue. Being in control of the field, and having survived the near disaster of the previous day, he was content to let the remaining Rebels go.[5]

Yet survival was insufficient for some Union officers, officials in the Lincoln administration, and editors in the northern press. Many decried the high casualties—over thirteen thousand Federals alone. Nevertheless, Grant had won an important, if narrow, victory at Shiloh, a victory that confirmed the Union's hold on western Tennessee and maintained the campaign's momentum. These achievements, however, would take time to recognize, in part because they were overshadowed by reports questioning Grant's leadership. His foremost critic was his fellow Union army commander Don Carlos Buell, who scoffed at the notion of a heroic Grant and instead condemned his leadership as limited to "indefinite or unimportant directions given without effect to straggling bodies of troops in the rear." Setting aside Buell's hyperbole, Grant's errors were numerous and, at times, egregious. In establishing his divisions at Pittsburg Landing, he allowed the greenest troops to pitch their tents at the southernmost point of the encampment, closest to the Confederates in Corinth, and without ordering the construction of field entrenchments, having stated a few months earlier that "drill and discipline is [*sic*] more necessary for the men than fortifications." He looked no farther than the closest tree line by failing to send out cavalry scouts, he ignored the repeated signs of an imminent Confederate attack, and he unwisely set up his headquarters nine miles from his army and on the opposite side of the Tennessee River. It comes as no surprise then that, at dawn on April 6, he was caught with his proverbial pants down. In the days immediately after the battle, he argued otherwise, claiming, "We could not have been better prepared had the enemy sent word three days before when they would attack. Skirmishing had been going on for that time and I could have brought on the battle either Friday [April 4] or Saturday if I had chosen. My object was to keep it off, if possible, until Buell arrived." While avoiding battle until united with Buell's army was sound strategic and tactical thinking, little evidence supports Grant's contention that he was aware of Johnston's approach.[6]

In his *Memoirs*, Grant continued to maintain that he had taken "every precaution . . . to keep advised of all movement of the enemy" and in this revealed something of his mind-set just prior to the battle. Outlining his view of the strategic situation, he described "the campaign we were engaged in as an offensive one and [I] had no idea that the enemy would leave strong intrenchments [*sic*] to take the initiative when he knew he would be attacked where he was if he remained." Here is perhaps the most severe error Grant committed at Shiloh. Again, as at both Belmont and Fort Donelson, he failed to anticipate the stratagems of his Confederate counterpart, and this time his lack of foresight nearly cost him not just a battle, but the very life of his army. His determination, which was now strong enough to carry him through the crisis of April 6 and order an attack for the following morning, had yet to develop the complex and sophisticated thinking necessary to anticipate or at a minimum take into account his opponent's actions. He had again focused exclusively on his plans, his objectives, and his movements, to the neglect of what his counterpart, a very capable Sidney Johnston, might do.[7]

Nevertheless, in this narrow Union victory there were positive signs of Grant's maturation as an army commander. With the steadying hand of Charles F. Smith gone, with his subordinate officers counseling withdrawal, and with his army all but defeated, on the night of April 6 Grant faced what was arguably the most critical combat crisis he would encounter during the war. In no other campaign did his command edge so near the precipice of annihilation. Yet that evening, sensing that the Confederates had exhausted themselves in the day's fighting and that the arrival of Buell's divisions gave him the advantage, he never considered retreat. His decision to stand firm was neither obstinate, impetuous, nor impulsive but rather a deliberate choice made under stress and against the recommendations of his staff. Grant had learned the lessons of earlier engagements: "So confident was I before firing ceased on the 6th that the next day would bring victory . . . if we could only take the initiative that I visited each division commander . . . [and] directed them . . . to engage the enemy as soon as found." Before the Union counterattack on April 7, Sherman recalled how Grant described the engagement at Fort Donelson, where, like now, "whoever assumed the offensive was sure to win." Grant's assessment was correct, and while critics might well argue that it came two days and thousands of casualties too late, his decision resurrected the fighting spirit of the army and its commanders.[8]

In the week or so after Shiloh, the armies tended to the scores of wounded. Thousands of casualties overwhelmed the ill-prepared medical staffs, while the grisly task of burying the dead created another kind of horror for the battle's survivors. On April 11, 1862, Halleck arrived on the field to take command of Grant's and Buell's armies and to direct operations against Corinth. Grant, no doubt still recovering from two exhausting days of battle, welcomed his arrival and his assumption of command. With the district commander present and the two Federal armies united, Grant hoped for a quick resumption of the campaign, but he did not account for Halleck's sluggish approach to war. "I am looking for a speedy move," he wrote his wife just days after Halleck arrived at Pittsburg Landing, "one more fight and then easy sailing to the close of the war. I really will feel glad when this thing is over." Instead, nearly two weeks passed before Halleck got the armies moving south, followed by another two weeks inching the twenty miles to Corinth. Grant strained at the snail's pace but was hesitant to criticize "Old Brains," even in letters to Julia: "We move slow Gen. Halleck being determined to make shure [sic] work."[9]

If Grant was reluctant to criticize, Halleck was not. On his arrival at Pittsburg Landing, he characterized Grant's army as "undisciplined and very much disorganized, the officers being utterly incapable of maintaining order." Halleck noted that soldiers took to firing their weapons indiscriminately, wasting precious powder and ammunition, and causing false alarms in an army anxious about surprise attacks. Even the paperwork in Grant's command did not meet Halleck's fastidious standards, provoking him to issue a directive: "Letters should relate to one matter only, and be properly folded and indorsed. Where the Regulations on this subject are not observed by officers, their communications to these Head Quarters will be returned." So Halleck went to work "to straighten things out," informing Grant, "Your army is not now in condition to resist an attack. It must be made so without delay."[10]

These perceived problems did nothing but confirm Halleck's suspicions of Grant's reputed incompetence. On April 30, again giving credence to the relentless rumors of Grant's drinking, Halleck elevated Grant to the impotent position of second in command, without any direct responsibility over troops. George H. Thomas, a division commander in Buell's Army of the Ohio, was given command of Grant's Army of the Tennessee. Promoted to irrelevance, or, as he described it, "my position differs but little from that of one in arrest," Grant asked Halleck for "either full restoration to duty, according to my rank, or to be relieved entirely from further duty." Halleck showed little inclination to do either, and as the days slipped by Grant nearly succumbed to depression and self-doubt, telling his wife, "I am seriously thinking of going home."[11]

Fate, as it is wont to do, then intervened with two events that saved Grant from resigning his commission. First, William T. Sherman, having heard that he was contemplating resignation, sought him out in his tent: "I found him seated on a camp-stool, with papers on a rude camp-table. . . . I inquired if it were true that he was going away. He said, 'Yes. . . . You know that I am in the way here. I have stood it as long as I can, and can endure it no longer.'" Sherman then reminded Grant of his own recent struggles, which included insinuations of mental instability, and assured him that this setback would likely prove temporary. Grant saw the wisdom in Sherman's words and decided to endure for at least a little while longer.[12]

Then, on June 10, came the second event that kept Grant in the army—Halleck reconsidered his "promotion" of Grant and decided to return him to command of the Army of the Tennessee. A month later, President Lincoln summoned Halleck to Washington to replace the recently fired George B. McClellan as general-in-chief, which allowed Grant to operate free of Halleck's incessant scrutiny, suspicions, and faultfinding. Sherman, who knew Grant better than anyone in the army, wrote to his friend on hearing of his decision to stay: "You could not be quiet at home for a week, when armies were moving, and rest could not relieve your mind of the gnawing sensation that injustice has been done you." Elihu Washburne, Grant's congressional patron, felt "great pleasure" when he heard of the general's return to command and was certain that "the confidence of your friends will be realized."[13]

Halleck had received a significant promotion, but Grant had won his own victory, surviving another political confrontation, and regaining command of, not only his army, but all Federal forces between the Mississippi and Tennessee Rivers, including the Army of the Mississippi, led by Gen. William S. Rosecrans. Sherman had been right. The setback had indeed been temporary, but in the interim Grant's resolve had faltered. It took the intervention of a trusted friend and a fortunate turn of events to keep him in the war, demonstrating that a great strength of will is neither innate nor permanent but instead requires vigilance, self-awareness, and occasional recommitment.[14]

By the summer of 1862, Grant had shown further development as a commander, and, while he had yet to recognize the importance of looking at a campaign from the perspective of the enemy, he had shown himself to be a tough, no-nonsense, determined fighter. His actions after the first day's fight at Shiloh exemplify the nature of Clausewitz's great force of will: "By the spark in his breast, by the light of his spirit, the spark of purpose, the light of hope, must be kindled afresh in others: in so far only as he is equal to this, he stands above the masses and continues to be their master."[15] The Grant of Shiloh was no longer the Grant who had approached Colonel Harris's Missouri encampment with trepidation and self-doubt. From that experience, from General Smith's mentoring, and from Belmont, Fort Henry, and Fort Donelson, he had developed a mental toughness whose mettle would be severely tested in campaigns yet to come.

Back in command, and with his headquarters in Memphis, Grant spent the last days of the 1862 summer searching for his next objective while playing a tug-of-war with Halleck to keep his forces together. The general-in-chief wanted the Federals in a smattering of posts from Memphis to Corinth and farther east, including the transfer of two of Grant's divisions to Buell's Army of the Ohio, now in Alabama. For Grant, with his command thinly spread across western Tennessee and northern Mississippi and unable to decipher Confederate intentions, this was "the most anxious period of the war." His anxiety was likely exacerbated by his recent differences with Halleck and being ordered to go on defense rather than follow his inclination to seize the initiative.[16]

If Halleck was not inclined to be aggressive, the Confederates were. As part of a three-pronged invasion of the North, Robert E. Lee's army marched into Maryland, while Braxton Bragg drove into Kentucky. In the West, the southern generals Sterling Price and Earl Van Dorn were to preoccupy Grant's men to prevent them from shifting east against Lee or Bragg. By mid-September, Grant anticipated an attack but looked to strike first, "disgusted" by news that one of his regiments had pulled back to the safety of Corinth rather than push forward to see what the Confederates were up to in nearby Iuka, Mississippi. After a summer of discontent, his confidence was back: "I expect to hold [Corinth] and have never had any other feeling either here or elsewhere but that of success."[17]

Price was indeed gathering in Iuka for an attack against the Yankees, but Grant beat him to the punch, issuing orders on September 18 to a division under Edward Ord and another under William Rosecrans to converge on the southerners the next day. He spurred Rosecrans to "make as rapid an advance as you can, and let us do tomorrow all we can." But tomorrow proved a great disappointment. Poor communication and coordination between the two division commanders allowed Price to slip away, leaving the Federals in possession of Iuka but having failed to do significant damage to the Confederates. Grant was frustrated, as was Rosecrans, who un-justly blamed Grant for failing to coordinate the converging Union divisions.[18]

While the Federal commanders fumed and pointed fingers, the southerners regrouped under Van Dorn, hoping to take back both the initiative and Corinth. Instead, by October 1, Grant had picked up on "a movement of the Rebels south of my front" and surmised that Corinth was their likely objective. Despite failing to achieve a decisive victory at Iuka, he again sought to reaffirm his momentum and "push those fellows to the wall." Van Dorn made the first move, striking the Federal defenses outside Corinth on October 3, but Grant was ready. Before the Confederates unleashed their assault, he shoved Rosecrans forward, sensing another chance to catch the southerners in the open: "We should attack if they do not. Do it soon. . . . Fight!" When word came that the battle was under way, he fired off telegrams to other commanders in the area, exhorting them to move to Corinth immediately. "Go with what you have got. . . . Rush as rapidly as possible," he cabled Gen. Stephen Hurlbut, who was ten or so miles away at Bolivar, Tennessee. By the end of the day, Van Dorn had fought his way to the outskirts of Corinth but, having failed to cap-ture the town, decided to renew the effort the next morning. Dawn roused the armies from their brief respite, and the battle resumed on October 4. The Confederates broke through to the town's critical rail junction, and for a fleeting moment victory seemed imminent, but Rosecrans led a counterattack, turning Van Dorn's Confederates out of Corinth. Commanding from centrally located Jackson, Tennessee, Grant telegraphed Rosecrans to keep the pressure on: "If the enemy fall back, push them with all force possible and save Hurlbut who is now on the way to your relief." The following morning at 8:00 A.M. in Washington, Halleck received word from Grant of a "great slaugh-ter" at Corinth, but Union forces still held the town, and Rosecrans was in pursuit of the retreating Rebels. Here was another opportunity to trap the enemy between Rosecrans and Hurlbut, a second chance for a decisive, if not mortal, blow against the southerners.[19]

There would be, however, no grand victory, at least not that day.

The Confederates fled north, eluding their pursuers, then turned south, skittering past Rosecrans to the safety of Holly Springs, Mississippi. Recognizing that the southerners had escaped, Grant called off the chase on October 7, telling Rosecrans, "We can do nothing with our weak forces but fall back to our old places. Order the pursuit to cease." That evening, Grant sent word to Halleck of his decision, drawing a rebuke from the usually cautious Halleck for his failure to offer chase: "Why order a return of your troops? Why not reinforce Rosecrans and pursue the enemy into Miss, supporting your army on the country?"[20]

Indeed, why not? An impatient Rosecrans was asking—in fact, demanding—a continuation of the offensive. He recommended Grant resupply Hurlbut, push him south, and order Sherman from Memphis with his entire force. Rosecrans's message reads more like an order than a request: "I repeat it is of the utmost importance to give the enemy no rest day or night but push him to Mobile & Jackson. . . . [N]ow is our time[.] [W]e must give the enemy no time to reinforce or recruit[.] Every nerve must be strained." A follow-up telegram from Rosecrans again took issue with Grant's reticence, displaying both insubordination and an uninformed, if not unrealistic, grasp of available resources and manpower. "I must deeply dissent," began the midnight telegram, "from your views as to the policy of pursuit. We have defeated routed and demoralized the army which holds the lower Miss Valley. . . . We have whipped them and should now push them to the wall. . . . I beseech you to send everything[.] Push them while they are broken hungry weary and illsupplied [*sic*]. Draw everything from Memphis to help move on Holly Springs. Let us concentrate and appeal to the Governors of the States to rush down twenty (20) or thirty (30) new Regiments." The vehemence of these requests gave Grant pause. He ordered Rosecrans to hold in place while he sought advice from Halleck and searched high and low for reinforcements. In the end, he could come up with only two regiments, not enough to sustain the chase, and the stop order held. Rosecrans, so incensed by Grant's apparent timidity and refusal to support an operation that, in his mind at least, could have bagged, not only the Confederate army, but Jackson and Mobile as well, requested a transfer from Grant's command.[21]

Was Rosecrans right? Did the general who had shown such resolve five months earlier at Shiloh suddenly lose his nerve, perhaps unwilling to risk failure so soon after his run-in with Halleck? Recall that immediately after the battle at Corinth Grant had ordered Rosecrans to pursue. Understandably, Rosecrans was unable to move quickly enough to trap the Rebels, given that his men had endured two days of some of the most intense fighting of the war. Van Dorn and his southerners dodged the Federals, crossing the Hatchie River on their way south, and at that point Grant realized: "[Rosecrans's men] could not have possibly caught the Enemy before reaching his fortifications at Holly Springs. . . . Our own troops would have suffered for food, and suffered greatly from fatigue." Clearly, Rosecrans disagreed, believing that a great victory had been lost. "If Grant had not stopped us," he wrote after the war, "we could have gone to Vicksburg. My judgment was to go on, and with the help suggested we could have done so. Under the pressure of a victorious force the enemy were experiencing all the weakening effects of a retreating army, whose means of supplies and munitions are always difficult to keep in order." True enough, but in these postwar recollections Rosecrans seems to have forgotten that his own army suffered from the same supply shortages, of which he had desperately informed Grant on October 9: "If forage is not sent us immediately our animals will die. This trip has worked them down and we have had sent us three hundred sacks. We require three thousand sacks per day. The case is critical and something must be done." *Something* must be done, but what? The necessary resources were not available, and, as the historian Brooks Simpson has observed, "to order a pursuit in such circumstances would risk too much."[22]

This episode marked the beginning of a long, strained, and uncooperative relationship between Rosecrans and Grant. Rosecrans's request for a transfer was granted in late October when Halleck tagged him to replace Don Carlos Buell as commander of the Army of the Ohio. Grant, at least ostensibly, bore no ill will, writing later,

"I was delighted at the promotion of General Rosecrans. . . . I still believed that when independent of an immediate superior the qualities which I, at the time, credited him with possessing, would show themselves."[23]

In the aftermath of the Battle of Corinth, Grant continued to demonstrate an analytical determination to press the fight, and his decisionmaking was increasingly marked by maturity and an informed reflection that distinguishes rational resolve from reckless zeal. Unwilling to risk an imprudent chase, as Rosecrans had advocated, he recognized the limitations of men and supplies and accepted the victory that his army had won. From Shiloh, Grant had come to recognize that this war would not be won with a single battle and that ultimate conquest would require thought, determination, and patience. Grant's command abilities had evolved and now included a strength of will tempered by a mind more attuned to the ever-changing nature of the battlefield. By midfall of 1862, in command of himself and his army, and having won two more battles, Grant went to work planning his next campaign, the capture of Vicksburg, the Confederate "Gibraltar of the West."

4

The Vicksburg Campaign

I am exceedingly anxious to do something.
—Ulysses S. Grant

By late October 1862, Grant was anticipating another Confederate drive to retake Corinth. Never happy surrendering the initiative to the enemy, he pushed Halleck to think more offensively. "You have never suggested to me any plan of opperations [*sic*] in this Department," he wrote from Jackson, Tennessee. "With small reinforcements at Memphis I think I would be able to move down the Mississippi Central [rail]road and cause the evacuation of Vicksburg." Abraham Lincoln believed that the city was the key to the western war effort, an opinion shared by his Confederate counterpart, Jefferson Davis, who described Vicksburg as "the nail head that holds the South's two halves together." With his simple proposal, Grant initiated what would become one of the war's great campaigns. It also revealed how Grant was underestimating the challenges that lay ahead for his men and his own leadership.[1]

Situated on soaring bluffs that tower over a hairpin turn in the Mississippi River, Vicksburg and its defenders presented a formidable obstacle to Union control of the river. Unassailable from the water, the town still had a potential weakness—its eastern approaches, roads that cut through deep ravines and passed under brooding southern earthworks. From November 1862 to the following March, Grant orchestrated a series of operations designed to place his army on the roads east of Vicksburg from which he could launch a direct assault. On November 2, five divisions set out from northern Mississippi on the first of these expeditions, a thrust along the Central Mississippi

Railroad toward Holly Springs, Grenada, and Jackson. The Federal troops would then make a hard turn to the west, toward Vicksburg. To Sherman, Grant wrote, "I am exceedingly anxious to do something before the roads get bad and before the enemy can entrench and reinforce." Once under way, Grant looked to increase his chances of success by sending Sherman with a separate force down the Mississippi River toward the city, thereby presenting Vicksburg's defender, Confederate general John C. Pemberton, with the dilemma of either splitting his forces or ignoring one of the two advancing Federal columns.[2]

Grant's now battle-tested army advanced southward at a steady pace, but its progress was short-lived. On December 20, Earl Van Dorn, having recovered from his thumping at Corinth two months earlier and now commanding cavalry troopers, descended on Grant's supply base at Holly Springs. He caught the Union guards by surprise and burned thousands of dollars' worth of goods. Grant hurried his own horse soldiers after the southerners, ordering Col. Benjamin Grierson to "pursue the enemy with all vigilance wherever they may go," but the damage had already been done, enough, in fact, that Grant turned the army around and headed back north. Meanwhile, Sherman's men fared no better. In late December, they failed to fight their way up the Chickasaw Bluffs onto dry ground north of the city. For Grant, these were tactical setbacks, and, although disappointing, they did not discourage him or dissuade him from pursuing his strategic objective of Vicksburg.[3]

As the new year began, Grant showed no signs of impatience or frustration with operations, though he did take exception to naysayers in the northern press who attacked his management of the campaign. "Grant," the *Chicago Tribune* editor Joseph Medill wrote to Congressman Washburne, "proves himself to be little better than a secesh." The general, for the most part, remained unperturbed by the criticism, but he complained to the sympathetic ear of his wife, Julia, "At present [some in the North] are behaving scandalously. . . . I want to see the Administration commence a war upon these people. They should suppress the disloyal press and confine during the war the noisy and most influential." More to the task at hand, to Halleck he reaffirmed that he would "do everything possible for the capture of Vicksburg" and explained, "To make a backward movement as long as that from Vicksburg to Memphis would be interpreted . . . as a defeat. . . . There was nothing left to be done but to *go forward to a decisive victory.*"[4]

Perhaps recognizing that the aborted drive through central Mississippi might give rise to doubt and defeatism, Grant focused his subordinates' eyes on the ultimate objective: Vicksburg. To McClernand he wrote, "This campaign must not fail. If there is force enough within the limits of my controll [*sic*] to secure a certain victory at Vicksburg they will be sent there." Brig. Gen. Willis A. Gorman, whose command was attached to McClernand's Thirteenth Corps, received a similar admonition: "The Mississippi River enterprise must take preecedence [*sic*] over all others and any side moves made must simply be to protect our flank and rear." At the same time, Grant was coming to the realization that the road to Vicksburg was not a road at all but a river. To get to dry land east of the city, the army would have to travel one of the innumerable rivers, streams, or bayous that crisscrossed the countryside like the veins of a leaf. There was no other way to wrest Vicksburg from the Confederates—"our troops must get below the city to be used effectively," and the only way to do that was by water. Then commenced a series of operations, some might say misadventures, all ostensibly designed to deposit a northern army on the eastern outskirts of the Confederate stronghold.[5]

To give each expedition the best chance, Grant kept his headquarters in the field to stay in close communication with his subordinate commanders. But the general's proximity failed to produce success as not one of the undertakings delivered a single Yankee soldier anywhere near the town. Through backwater bayous, Louisiana swamps, Mississippi rivers, and canals dug through a fog of mosquitoes, the bluecoats labored from late winter into early spring, always moving forward but in the end arriving no closer to their goal than when they started. Grant grew increasingly irritated and restless with each passing day:

February 11: "We are not much nearer an attack on Vicksburg now apparently than when I first come down."

February 27: "The everlasting rains set us back here wonderfully in our work. It is impossible for us to get done more than one days [*sic*] work in three."

March 27: "I am very well but much perplexed. Heretofore I have had nothing to do but fight the enemy. This time I have to overcome obsticles [*sic*] to reach him."

Nevertheless, Grant maintained his optimism and focus on the primary objective: "Foot once upon dry land on the other side of the [Mississippi] river I think the balance would be of but short duration." After the war, he maintained that at the time he had no real expectation that any of these operations would be successful, that he had the ulterior objective of keeping the men occupied. "Then commenced a series of experiments," he wrote in his memoirs, "to consume time, and to divert the attention of the enemy, of my troops and of the public generally. I, myself, never felt great confidence that any of the experiments resorted to would prove successful. Nevertheless I was always prepared to take advantage of them in case they did." While this certainly rings of postwar spin, Confederate major Samuel H. Lockett, chief engineer for the Department of Mississippi and East Louisiana, who monitored these Federal false starts with an opponent's critical eye, gives credence to Grant's contention, noting, "Though these expeditions all failed, the desperate nature of most of them convinced us that General Grant was in deep earnest, and not easily discouraged." Operationally, the winter and spring had produced little in the way of demonstrable returns for the wealth of time and energy invested, but, by keeping the army active and himself engaged, the Union commander had still won a victory of sorts.[6]

Yet Grant remained outside Vicksburg looking in, and everyone knew it. Northern newspapers resurrected the rumors of drink and clamored for his relief, while Cadwallader Washburn, the brother of

Grant's congressional patron Elihu and a cavalry officer in the Thirteenth Corps, opined, "This campaign is being wholly mismanaged. All of Grant's schemes have failed. He knows that he has got to do something or off goes his head." Having exhausted what seemed to be every possible option, Grant looked for assistance from the navy, as he had done during the Forts Henry and Donelson campaign. Flag Officer Henry Foote's Fort Donelson wound had continued to fester, keeping him from active service, so Rear Adm. David Dixon Porter, a determined leader in his own right, had taken Foote's place. Son of a War of 1812 naval hero, and destined for a sixty-one-year career, Porter was no stranger to joint operations. He had worked with the army on a number of occasions, including Winfield Scott and his amphibious landing at Vera Cruz in 1847, Capt. Montgomery C. Meigs and the reinforcement of Fort Pickens, Florida, in 1861, and John McClernand at Fort Hindman, Arkansas, just months earlier in January 1863. Porter was now in command of the Mississippi River Squadron and was anxious to cooperate with Grant. Working together, the two drafted a daring plan that, if successful, would quiet Grant's critics and deliver his men to the promised land of high, dry ground east of Vicksburg. The foot soldiers would march south along the western side of the Mississippi, while Porter's squadron, under the cover of darkness, would try to slip past the city's artillery-studded bluffs. If successful, soldiers and sailors would meet south of the city, where Porter's transports could ferry the army across the river to a landing on the eastern bank. Vicksburg would then, finally, be within reach.[7]

As twilight gave way to darkness on April 16, north of the city Porter's fleet loosed their moorings and began to drift south on the river's current, lights extinguished, engines at a low idle to keep noise to a minimum. They swung around the bend in the river, slipping toward the ominous black bluffs on the left. Then a single cannon shot rang out. Within minutes, Confederate batteries roared to life. Artillery shells targeted the parade of Union gunboats, coal barges, and empty troop transports a hundred feet below. Some shells whistled over the crouching Union sailors; others found their mark. A few hours later, Yankee sailors celebrated their unexpected good luck while Rebel gunners cursed their poor shooting as the barrage had dealt little substantial damage to the squadron. All but one of the gunboats and transports had survived the hair-raising passage, the transport ship *Henry Clay* being the lone exception, and they could now move to meet Grant's soldiers a few miles south on the west bank. From his flagship, the *Benton,* Porter sent word to Grant, "This move has demoralized these fellows very much, dont [*sic*] give them time to get over it." As with Foote during the Fort Donelson campaign, Grant had found in Porter a naval commander who shared his philosophy of relentless war.[8]

With the transports safely past Vicksburg's artillery, Grant set about finding a location to make the river crossing. Despite a strong Confederate presence, Grand Gulf, about thirty miles south of Vicksburg, presented the best option. Grant told Sherman of his hopes that Grand Gulf would "easily fall" if struck quickly; however, he harbored no false optimism: "I foresee great difficulties in our present position, but it will not do, to let these retard any movement." He did not let his desire for quick action blind him to the risks of attacking Grand Gulf, which, while no Vicksburg, had its own southern defenders perched on river-view bluffs. To draw the Confederates' attention elsewhere, he ordered Sherman to make a demonstration north of Vicksburg against Haynes Bluff, and, to keep in check his aggressive subordinate, he made clear that this was to be a demonstration *only,* not a full attack. Grant's planning came to naught, however, when on April 29 Confederate gunners at Grand Gulf stopped cold a preliminary bombardment attempted by Porter's gunboats. Grant decided that Grand Gulf was "as defensible upon its front as Vicksburg and . . . just as impossible to capture by a front attack." Another obstacle, another frustration, another delay, but Grant adapted his plans and turned away from Grand Gulf in search of a more favorable crossing point.[9]

With the momentum of Porter's night passage slipping away, Grant sought to make a second attempt at transiting the river as rapidly as possible. In less than twenty-four hours, a new landing site, Bruinsburg, Mississippi, had been chosen. Federal soldiers scanned the eastern banks of the river for Confederates as Porter's transports ferried them across. Gen. John McClernand's Thirteenth Corps led the advance and met not a single southerner, thanks to a combination of Sherman's earlier demonstration at Haynes Bluff and a Union cavalry raid Grant had ordered two weeks earlier. Col. Benjamin Grierson and his seventeen hundred troopers had departed from the Mississippi-Tennessee state line on April 16, the same day the navy floated past Vicksburg, with their course set south. Over the next two weeks, they covered six hundred miles, destroying railroads and supplies along the way before riding into Baton Rouge, Louisiana, exhausted but jubilant at their success. As Grant had hoped, from Sherman, to Grierson, to Grant himself, Confederate commanders did not know who posed the greatest or the most imminent threat. Late in the evening of May 1, as naval transports shuttled Yankee invaders across the river and McClernand's men marched inland toward the town of Port Gibson, Grant sent a message to Admiral Porter that celebrated—at least as much as the general was ever inclined to celebrate—their success: "Our day's work has been very creditable. . . . Our forces are on the move, and will lie very close to Port Gibson tonight—ready for early action tomorrow. Grierson of the cavalry, has taken the heart out of Mississippi."[10]

Standing on the eastern bank of the river, Grant paused to reflect on his army's success, born of determination and perseverance: "I was now in the enemy's country, with a vast river and the stronghold of Vicksburg between me and my base of supplies. But I was on dry ground on the same side of the river with the enemy. All the campaigns, labors, hardships and exposures . . . that had been made and endured, were for the accomplishment of this one object." The army would have to operate on a tenuous supply line, but he was on the eastern side of the Mississippi, with only Confederate soldiers blocking his entry into Vicksburg, admittedly no small obstacle. If he had yet to defeat the enemy, he had at least conquered the enemy's greatest ally—the geography of Mississippi.[11]

Grant now sought to instill his own confidence and tenacity in those who served both above and below him. As the army pushed inland, he assured Halleck in Washington, "This is a long and pre-carious route but I have every confidence in succeeding in doing it. . . . [We will] not stop until Vicksburg is in our possession." As for the men who would do the fighting in the coming days, they had through the trials and privations of the past winter developed a trust in their commander, not the fleeting parade-ground adulation sought by a George McClellan, but a sober respect that mirrored their general's own understated determination. He had pushed his soldiers, and they had responded, "march[ing] as much by night as by day, through mud and rain, without tents or much other baggage, and on irregular rations, without complaint and with less straggling than I have ever before witnessed."[12]

Now in Mississippi, Grant knew that hesitation or delay would court disaster. Lt. Gen. John C. Pemberton's Vicksburg army, which had been applying pick and shovel to the city's already formidable earthworks, was on the move to head off the blue column. Looking to give Pemberton an even stronger hand, Confederate forces near Jackson were adding recruits, motivated by the clear and unmistak-able threat Grant posed. Conversely, the Federals could expect no reinforcements and, more significant, had cut themselves off from all but a mere trickle of supplies hauled down the Mississippi's muddy western bank and then ferried across the river. Sherman advised an operational pause before setting the army in motion, but Grant was not about to give up the initiative that was so long in coming. All the "horses, mules, or oxen in the vicinity" were immediately sworn into the U.S. Army and "loaded to their capacity with ammunition." His men would have to fight on a minimum of supplies, "rations of hard bread, coffee, and salt," supplemented by whatever else the farms of Mississippi might offer up. Grant intended to move fast, to move light, and to do it now.[13]

The success of the operation would ultimately depend on Grant's determination to see it through. With Sherman, his most trusted subordinate, harboring grave doubts about this venture, Grant had his work cut out for him. Earlier in April, before Porter's fleet had made its night passage of Vicksburg, Sherman had recommended withdrawing north and making a second attempt at driving through central Mississippi, along the path Grant had tried the previous December. Grant let the idea die without comment. He had no interest in backtracking. Now, with the army south of Vicksburg and poised to strike, Sherman remained recalcitrant, Grant later recalling him saying "that I was putting myself in a position voluntarily which an enemy would be glad to maneuver [*sic*] a year—or a long time—to get me in." If Grant had any such reservations, he shared them with no one; he had spent the last five months pressing his men down every possible avenue to get to this very point. Now he was right where he wanted to be.[14]

As the bluecoats continued to file off Porter's transports on the evening of May 1, Grant sent orders to John McClernand, pressing his lead corps commander to be relentless: "Push the enemy with skirmishers well thrown out, till it gets too dark to see him. . . . [R]enew the attack at early dawn and if possible push the enemy from the field or capture him." The next day, as McClernand closed in on Port Gibson, Grant received a message from Confederate brigadier general John S. Bowen, the competent, respected, and now unfortunate commander of the only Rebel force immediately available to contest the Federal advance. Bowen asked for a "twenty four hours suspension of hostilities" to minister to the previous day's wounded, but Grant rejected the request out of hand. "A dispatch now in my possession," read his reply, "shows that you are expecting reinforcements and additional munitions of war. I deem therefore the request unreasonable and one you could not expect me to comply with." As Bowen and the other Confederate high command would soon learn, their Yankee opponent had no intention of suspending this campaign for any reason.[15]

The Federals' superior numbers overwhelmed in short order what Grant described as Bowen's "very bold" defense of Port Gibson. Although the Confederates could not hold the town, during their withdrawal north they managed to destroy the bridges over Bayou Pierre, a meandering waterway that cut across Grant's intended line of march. Union engineers immediately set about bridging

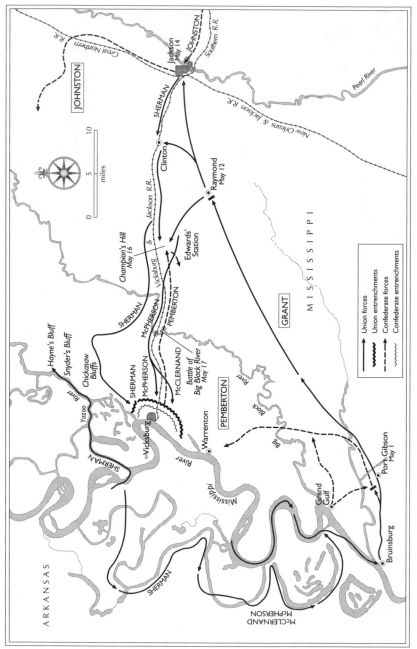

Map 2. The Vicksburg campaign

the bayou as Grant worked up plans to get James B. McPherson's and McClernand's corps moving again. He was initially inclined to bring the army to Grand Gulf, likely to refit for the fight that was soon to come, but, showing the same adaptability and determination to keep the initiative as he had during the Forts Henry and Donelson campaign, he decided to "immediately follow the enemy, and if all promises as favorably hereafter as it does now, not stop until Vicksburg is in our possession." As the army prepared to move out of Port Gibson, Grant paused a moment to watch the engineers working to span the bayou, including the officer in charge, Col. J. H. Wilson, whom he could not help but notice "going into the water and working as hard as any one engaged." The scene must have taken the army commander back to another time, when during the Mexican War a young lieutenant worked feverishly in the water and drew the attention of his commanding general, Zachary Taylor.[16]

On May 3, 1863, the Army of the Tennessee stepped off on its march to Vicksburg, an operation that had been nearly five months in the making. Charles A. Dana, a War Department official sent west to monitor—some might have said to spy on—Grant, reported back to his chief, Secretary of War Stanton, "General Grant intends to lose no time in pushing his army toward the Big Black Bridge and Jackson, threatening both and striking at either, as is most convenient." Grant himself was in high spirits, informing Sherman, "The enemy is badly beaten, greatly demoralized and exhausted of ammunition. The road to Vicksburg is open; all we want now are men, ammunition and hard bread." He further directed Sherman to "hurry up, cross [the Mississippi] at Grand Gulf, and hurry forward." The enemy, however, was not in such poor straits as Grant thought, and the simple needs of men, ammunition, and bread were not so easily satisfied. Giving credence to the old army adage that professionals are more concerned with logistics than tactics, Grant focused squarely on supplying his men with sufficient provisions to avoid delay. To Sherman he acknowledged the impossibility of bringing up full rations: "[But] what I do expect . . . is to get up what rations of hard bread, coffee and salt we can and make the country furnish the balance. . . . A delay would give the enemy time to reinforce and fortify." He therefore sent orders back to his supply base at Grand Gulf, directing the commissary officers to move with "the greatest promptness" and, if necessary, relieve any dilatory officers. When at one point insufficient supplies slowed the army's progress, he placed the responsibility directly on the quartermaster department, something he was familiar with from his days in the prewar army: "Movements here are delayed for want of Ammunition and stores. Every days [*sic*] delay is worth two thousand men to the enemy." Despite his frustrations with the slow start, Grant took a moment on May 7 to issue General Order No. 32, in which he thanked his men for their capture of Port Gibson but warned, "More difficulties and privations are before us. Let us endure them manfully. Other battles are to be fought. Let us fight them bravely." The men had fought well, momentum was on their side, and they would give the enemy no respite.[17]

Grant's initial plan was to move north from Port Gibson to the Big Black River, effect a crossing wherever possible, and then strike out directly for Vicksburg. By May 6, the army had reached the Big Black, and there Grant demonstrated the difference between unthinking stubbornness and analytical determination. Word came of a Confederate force collecting about forty-five miles east of Vicksburg in the vicinity of Jackson, also the location of the critical junction of the Mississippi Central and Southern rail lines. If the Rebels were indeed able to cobble together a viable force, Grant's army could find itself between that hammer and the anvil of Vicksburg. A less adept commander might have opted for what appeared to be a quick and easy solution: push on as rapidly as possible, hoping to secure Vicksburg before the gathering Confederates could swing the hammer. An irresolute general may well have stalled the campaign to marshal additional resources and reinforcements. Instead, while keeping an eye on the objective of Vicksburg, Grant identified the southerners near Jackson as the most serious threat and decided "to move swiftly towards Jackson, destroy or drive any force in that direction and then turn" back toward Vicksburg.[18]

Within a few days, the bluecoats had pushed deep into Mississippi, heading northeast toward Jackson with Maj. Gen. James McPherson's Seventeenth Corps in the van. On May 12, at the small town of Raymond, about twenty miles from Jackson, Brig. Gen. John Gregg mustered a brigade's worth of Confederates into a line of battle, dead set on denying the Yankees possession of the town, thinking that he faced a flank guard rather than a full corps. The outcome was never in doubt. McPherson's midwesterners swamped the southern defenses before spilling into the town, where they enjoyed the picnic that townspeople had set out in anticipation of a victory celebration.[19] As surviving Confederates beat a lively retreat toward Jackson, Grant notified his corps commanders that he wanted no letup; move toward Clinton just west of Jackson on the rail line, then strike directly for the city and the Rebels. Just after midnight on May 14, as Sherman approached the outskirts of Jackson, Grant informed McPherson, "Sherman will push on as rapidly as possible. . . . We must get Jackson or as near it as possible to-night." Later that day, the Yankees did fight their way into the state capital, shoving the Confederates, under the command of Gen. Joseph E. Johnston, out of the city and north toward Canton. Johnston then assumed the role of a frustrated, fidgety, and impotent bystander for the rest of the campaign. As was the case two days earlier after the battle at Raymond, Grant wanted no letup. He had the initiative and was going to make the most of it. "Turn all your forces [to the west] towards Bolton station and make all dispatch in getting there. Move troops by the most direct road from wherever they may be on the receipt of this order," he ordered McClernand and Maj. Gen. Francis P. Blair, one of Sherman's division commanders. Before the evening hours of May 14 had slipped away, the Union army was on the move again, this time heading west toward Vicksburg.[20]

By the morning of May 16, Grant sensed opportunity; Pemberton had brought the bulk of his army out of Vicksburg's defenses in the forlorn hope of linking up with Joe Johnston. The day was just beginning when the two armies made contact about halfway between Jackson and Vicksburg near high ground known as Champion Hill. Over the course of the day, and through some of the heaviest fighting in the campaign, Rebel and Yankee went after each other with a grim determination characteristic of veteran soldiers. Early on, Grant was at the front, where he maneuvered forces, including positioning individual artillery batteries to block a Confederate advance. By late afternoon, despite the failure of John McClernand to strike the exposed flank of the enemy, the Federals began to overwhelm the southerners and force Pemberton's line to dissolve into a chaotic retreat.[21]

As the Confederates streamed westward, Grant spent the remainder of the afternoon and evening orchestrating the operation that he hoped would deliver the coup de grâce to Pemberton's fleeing army. If it could be caught before reaching the safety of Vicksburg's earthworks, both time and lives could be saved. He got word to two division commanders, Peter Osterhaus and Eugene Carr, to "pursue vigorously as far as the Big Black [River], and to cross it" if they could. Francis Blair, another division commander, received orders from Grant to "move at early dawn toward Black River bridge" and engage the enemy at once if encountered. To Sherman, still with the bulk of his corps in the army's rear near Jackson, Grant relayed news of the day's "desperate fight": "The enemy were driven and are now in full retreat. I am of the opinion that the battle of Vicksburg has been fought. We must be prepared however for whatever turns up. McClernand and McPherson are in full pursuit and will continue until night closes in. I want you to advance as far as possible tonight and start early in the morning again." As the evening wore on, Grant formulated a plan to send Sherman's force north of the Big Black River bridge in anticipation of moving around Pemberton's left flank while McClernand and McPherson fixed the southerners at the bridge. In response to these new orders, Sherman replied, "You may count on my being across in three hours." He then inquired whether he should move into the city if the opportunity presented itself, to which Grant not surprisingly answered, "If . . . you can go immediately into the city do so," sharing his hope to "either have Vicksburg or Hains [sic] Bluff [north of town overlooking the Mississippi River] tomorrow night." A bit optimistic perhaps, but Grant believed that he had the Confederates on the run and that by driving forward he could end the campaign sooner rather than later.[22]

The heavy fighting on May 17 took place, not in Sherman's front, but at the bridges on the main road to Vicksburg, where three Confederate brigades fanned out in a defensive arc on the east side of the river. Carr's Union division made initial contact, with Brig. Gen. Michael Lawler's brigade of Iowans getting first crack at the Rebels. Lawler's men did their work expeditiously, driving the southerners across the river, but not fast enough to prevent them from firing the bridges. Almost as soon as the last Confederate disappeared to the west, the sound of Union engineers' tools could be heard as three new bridges began to reach from the east bank to the west. Grant pushed corps commanders McClernand and McPherson to get their men across as quickly as possible, leaving all baggage to follow later except for ambulances and ammunition. The next morning, the Army of the Tennessee was once again in pursuit of its fleeing opponent. Disappointed that the southerners had again escaped, the Federals were still hopeful.[23]

As Grant was watching the battle at the Big Black, a rider appeared bearing orders that had the potential to derail the entire campaign. Originating from Halleck in Washington, the orders came by way of Maj. Gen. Nathaniel P. Banks, the commander of the Union forces besieging the other Confederate stronghold on the Mississippi at Port Hudson, Louisiana, about 110 miles to the south. Grant was ordered to break contact with the enemy, return immediately to Grand Gulf, and then proceed south to cooperate with Banks in the capture of Port Hudson. Earlier in the campaign, Grant had entertained the possibility of supporting Banks prior to moving against Vicksburg, but on May 10, as his troops advanced deep into Mississippi, he sent word to Port Hudson that, as he later recalled, "I . . . could not afford to retrace my steps." Now Grant had clear orders from the Union general-in-chief directing him to do just that. Grant's answer was an unequivocal no; he had come too far and was too close to his objective to be turned aside by an order that was out of date and inappropriate for the current battlefield situation: "I told the officer that the order came too late, and that Halleck would not give it now if he knew of our position." The officer, Brig. Gen. William Dwight, one of Banks's staff officers, wanted to debate the matter, but at that moment Lawler's advance against the Confederates grew hot and drew Grant back to the fight. Banks would remain on his own while Grant continued the drive toward Vicksburg.[24]

From May 12 through May 17, the Army of the Tennessee had fought and won four engagements and prevented Pemberton's and Johnston's Confederate armies from uniting, significant accomplishments by any measure. Nevertheless, Grant had failed to strike a fatal blow before the southerners withdrew into Vicksburg. Still, he hoped for a quick and decisive victory. Believing Pemberton's men had to be demoralized after their recent drubbings, Grant was not about to let them settle in and improve their fortifications unmolested. Much of the Federal army was still strung out on the road back toward the Big Black River and Champion Hill, suffering from the previous seven days of hard marches punctuated by fierce fights. Despite the army's fatigue, on May 19 Grant ordered Sherman's Fifteenth Corps to test the Confederates' resolve and defenses, even though they could expect little support from the trailing corps of McClernand and McPherson. At two o'clock in the afternoon, three artillery shots in rapid succession signaled the beginning of the assault, and Sherman's men moved out in line of battle northeast of the city, adjacent to the Graveyard and Jackson Roads. Advancing from the concealment of trees and ridge lines, Illinois, Ohio, and Missouri infantry met a hail of musket and artillery fire as they made their way down one hundred feet and more into vine- and tree-choked ravines. From the bottom, the men then scaled the opposite slope to the top of the next ridge, where they hit the Confederates' network of mutually supporting fortifications. Regulars from the First Battalion, Thirteenth U.S. Regiment, planted their flags on the escarpment of the Stockade Redan but could advance no farther. The Yankee attack had played out, not coming close to cracking the southern defenses, let alone achieving a decisive breakthrough. By nightfall, the survivors were picking their way over the dead back to the safety of their own lines.[25]

Grant was not ready to give up. The operations of May 19 could be described in today's terms as a hasty attack, an assault made on an enemy who appears unprepared to mount a substantial defense, even though the attack may lack for sufficient planning and preparation. Sherman had failed to punch through, but the Confederates might crack if the weight of the entire Union army was thrown at them in a coordinated charge along the length of the line. A simultaneous attack would deny the defenders the advantage of interior lines, and, if there was a weak point in the defenses, an all-out assault would surely expose it. On May 21, Grant issued orders for an attack to commence at ten o'clock the following morning, "by all the Army corps of this Army." The next day, after a lengthy artillery barrage the Yankees pressed forward. As Sherman's men moved out over the same ground they had bloodied three days earlier, McPherson's and McClernand's men discovered for themselves that Vicksburg's terrain seemed to be in a conspiracy with the Confederates to keep them out of the city. Sherman's regiments advanced no farther than in their earlier attack, but in the early afternoon Iowans in McClernand's corps had clawed their way into a Rebel redoubt near where the Southern Railroad snaked through the lines. A spirited counterattack by Texas infantry, however, dashed any hopes the Yankees had for an evening celebration in Vicksburg. Two days of battering against impregnable Confederate defenses had done little but add to the Federals' casualty count.[26]

One might criticize Grant for ordering these two assaults, especially the second, evidence that he was overly aggressive in his decisionmaking. The first attack was undertaken with little planning and with no knowledge of Confederate dispositions. Moreover, it was executed by only a third of his army, which was exhausted from a relentless campaign tempo. The second attack, although including all three corps, faced an enemy secure in fortifications on bluffs that commanded nearly ideal fields of fire. Grant, it would appear, had let his desire to gain Vicksburg cloud reasoned judgment.

The evidence, however, points to a commander who based his decisions on previous experience and whose analytical reasoning was more sophisticated than first glance might suggest. In his general orders of May 21 calling for coordinated attacks, he expressed his belief that a vigorous offensive would "carry Vicksburg in a very short time and with very much less loss than would be sustained by delay. Every days [*sic*] enables the enemy to strengthen his defences [*sic*] and increases his chances for receiving aid from outside." His first point needs little elaboration; until the southern defenses were tested, there was no way to know whether they were a thin crust ready to crack or an impervious barrier. Concerning his second point, in his memoirs Grant points out that Johnston's Confederate force was still hovering north of Jackson within fifty miles of Vicksburg and was likely receiving a steady, if not significant, influx of reinforcements. Even if Johnston did not pose a fatal threat to the Army of the Tennessee, he could still derail Grant's efforts to capture Vicksburg and Pemberton's thirty thousand Rebels. The sooner Vicksburg was in Union hands, the fewer opportunities Johnston would have to reenter the game.[27]

If we look beyond Grant's own explanations penned years after the war and place the assaults of May 19 and 22 in the context of his experiences and his development as a commander, we can see that his decisionmaking was informed, not by a lack of critical thinking, but by the lessons he had learned throughout his career. At Molino del Ray in 1847 during the Mexican War, he saw that the failure to follow up immediately a successful attack in front of Chapultepec meant "five days later more valuable lives were sacrificed to carry works which had been so nearly in our possession. . . . It is always [appropriate] to follow a retreating foe, unless stopped or otherwise directed." He demonstrated that commitment to keeping the initiative in the advance on Fort Donelson in early 1862, when he saw that his army of fifteen thousand would be more effective at that moment than a host of fifty thousand a month later. At Vicksburg, he also confirmed that he had learned something else at Fort Donelson, a lesson reinforced at Shiloh, that, when both armies are disorganized, confused, and exhausted, the one who attacks first will most likely emerge victorious.[28]

Further evidence that Grant had carried out something of a risk/benefit analysis prior to the two assaults was his decision to undertake siege operations immediately after the failed May 22 attack. There would be no more all-out assaults; instead, the Federals would "out-camp the enemy," as Grant described the coming siege. Even as Union troops began digging trenches on May 23, Grant informed Admiral Porter of this new strategy and the thinking behind it: "There is no doubt of the fall of this place ultimately but how long it will take is a matter of doubt. I intend to lose no more men but to force the enemy from one position to another without exposing my troops." To Gen. Nathaniel P. Banks, operating in Louisiana, he explained his decision as the best way to take the city and "save my men." Grant later maintained that the two aborted attacks were necessary to convince both officers and men that the hard, tedious work of a prolonged siege was necessary; perhaps that was so, but more likely the setbacks of May 19 and 22 were necessary to convince Grant himself that Vicksburg would fall, not to rifle and cannon, but only to the pick and shovel. Kicking down the door was worth a try, even two, but, when the southerners blocked each thrust, Grant, as he had done repeatedly in the past, shifted to a new strategy while keeping his focus on the ultimate objective.[29]

Grant finally had his army at Vicksburg, admittedly not in the city, but that would come in due time. As he gazed down on the Mississippi River from the bluffs north of the city, he was joined by Sherman, who had been skeptical of the operation from the river crossing on May 1. Grant later recalled: "[Sherman confessed] that up to this minute he had felt no positive assurance of success. This, however, he said was the end of one of the greatest campaigns in history and I ought to make a report of it at once. Vicksburg was not yet captured, and there was no telling what might happen before it was taken; but whether captured or not, this was a complete and successful campaign." A successful campaign indeed and one that clearly illustrates Grant's perseverance, adaptability, and aversion to surrendering the initiative. The newspaperman Sylvanus Cadwallader had traveled with the army as they fought their way first to Jackson, then to the outskirts of Vicksburg, and on May 16, the day of the clash at Champion Hill, he posted a letter home. "I have been riding day and night throughout this campaign," he wrote to his wife. "The army is absolutely nomadic. We march and fight alternately." Writing after the war, Cadwallader described Grant's existence on the road as no-nonsense and Spartan. Always at the front, pushing his corps commanders to pursue the enemy, the general shared in the deprivations of hard campaigning, "depending on borrowed horses for passing from one command to another, sleeping on the ground without blankets or covering of any kind; and having no baggage but a toothbrush." Indeed, earlier in the campaign, during the lull that followed the capture of Port Gibson on May 3, was the first chance Grant had in six days "to get a bath, borrow some fresh underclothing from one of the naval officers, and get a good meal." The manner in which Grant conducted this campaign made evident the ongoing evolution of his approach to war fighting: relentless pursuit of an objective through adaptive, analytical determination.[30]

On May 25, Grant issued orders to the corps commanders formalizing the army's new strategy of siege warfare: "Immediately commence the work of reducing the enemy by regular approaches. It is desirable that no more loss of life shall be sustained in the reduction of Vicksburg, and the capture of the Garrison." Having reestablished his lines of communication when he reached Vicksburg on May 18, Grant reassured General Halleck and thereby President Lincoln, "The enemy are now undoubtedly in our grasp. The fall of Vicksburg, and the capture of most of the garrison, can only be a question of time." For Grant, this was no false or ill-founded confidence; a secure and efficient supply line was shuttling both goods and men down the Mississippi, bulking up a veteran army that was fully prepared for whatever the Confederates might try.[31]

Keeping tabs on Pemberton's men was easy; Grant had them penned up in the city between his army to the east and Porter's gunboat fleet on the river to the west. Johnston's force back in the vicinity of Jackson was more difficult to track, and, while chastened by their earlier scrape with the Yankees, they remained dangerous. In late May, as Union engineers began laying out their approach trenches, Grant sent cavalry troopers out to monitor the southerners, and soon after he posted infantry at key positions along the Big Black River and towns to the east to protect the back of his siege lines. This time he would not be caught unaware as at Shiloh: "I will avoid a surprise and do the best I can with all the means at hand." By late June, Grant had sufficient combat power to create a second line under Sherman that faced east, initially consisting of five brigades, with another eleven thousand men available if needed. Grant had avoided becoming so consumed with the prize in his front that he ignored the threat of Johnston to his rear.[32]

John Pemberton's besieged army would gain no relief from Joseph E. Johnston, nor would Nathaniel Banks at Port Hudson receive reinforcements from Grant, who on May 25 sent Banks word that siege operations were under way at Vicksburg. A week later, Grant expressed his regrets, but "the circumstances by which I am surrounded will prevent my making any detachments at this time." He reminded Banks that "Vicksburg is the vital point" and that "we have after great labor and extraordinary risk secured a position which should not be jeopardized by any detachments whatever." A month later, both generals were still locked in their respective sieges, anticipating a breakthrough sooner rather than later, and Grant had not budged in his refusal to shift troops south to Banks. The capture of Vicksburg, he assured Banks, would leave "me able to send you any force that might be required against Port Hudson," but, until that time, the Army of the Tennessee was staying right where it was.[33]

Up to this point, Grant had conducted the siege well, overseeing the progress of the approach trenches, monitoring for threats from the rear, and maintaining communications with his commander and other generals in the region. As a result, even though he had yet to secure Vicksburg, his reputation as a fighter grew. Maj. Gen. Benjamin Prentiss, Grant's division commander at Shiloh, whom he had tasked with holding the center "at all hazards," sent word of support from Arkansas: "I feel altogether sanguine and confident of the result. My only regret is that I am not permitted to be with you." An army captain in St. Louis acknowledged to Grant's chief of staff, John Rawlins, "You have a gigantic work to accomplish but I tell

every one that Grant never was whipped and never means to be."
Nevertheless, by mid-June 1863, operations at Vicksburg had been
going on for nearly four weeks, and leaders in Washington were becoming impatient, or at least General Halleck was, fairly ironic given
the ponderous pace at which he had conducted his own campaigns in
the past. "I hope you fully appreciate," he telegraphed Grant on June
12, "the importance of *time* in the reduction of Vicksburg. The large
reenforcements [*sic*] sent to you have opened Missouri and Kentucky
to rebel raids. The seige [*sic*] should be pushed night and day with all
possible despatch [*sic*]." Halleck's concern was likely exacerbated by
the recent movement of Robert E. Lee's Army of Northern Virginia,
all signs indicating that the Rebels had every intention of heading
north into Maryland, if not Pennsylvania. Grant, of course, needed
little prodding as he was keeping the pressure on his subordinates
to push forward. In one instance, on June 16, he directed a division commander in McPherson's corps, Maj. Gen. Francis Herron,
to "push forward . . . as rapidly as possible towards the enemy's lines
establishing your batteries on the most commanding positions as you
advance."[34]

During the Vicksburg siege, two troublesome issues arose that
necessitate a brief exploration given that both had the potential to
disrupt operations: Grant's handling of the prickly John McClernand
and the commanding general's relationship with alcohol. Despite
having served together for nearly a year and a half, Grant and Mc-
Clernand had rarely gotten along, at best tolerating each other. Mc-
Clernand was first and foremost a hard-driving politician who, while
no Napoléon, showed hints of military competence; nevertheless, he
saw battlefield victories as the best way to advance his political career,
ultimately, he hoped, to the presidency. Grant, on the other hand,
was a hard-driving general who showed no interest in elected office
(at least during the war) and saw Union victories as the only way
to end the conflict and maintain the Union. Historians have doc-
umented this rocky relationship, which need not be fully rehashed
here. Suffice it to say, McClernand irritated more than just Grant,
including Charles A. Dana, the eyes and ears of Secretary of War Ed-

win Stanton, and, most important, General-in-Chief Henry Halleck. By January 1863, Grant had initial approval from both Stanton and Halleck to relieve McClernand, and in May Stanton reassured Grant of the same, with the added warning of consequences for *not* removing incompetents: "General Grant has full and absolute authority to enforce his own commands, and to remove any person who . . . interferes with, or delays his operations. . . . [H]e will be responsible for any failure to exert his powers." As the army fought its way from Port Gibson to Jackson to Vicksburg, Grant had sought to keep distractions at a minimum and was hesitant to act against McClernand without a clear sign from Washington that his removal was politically acceptable. Then in late May, when the campaign settled into siege operations, McClernand made a fatal misstep. In violation of standing orders, he had published in an Illinois newspaper a pronouncement congratulating his corps for their performance in the May 22 assault, praise that unfairly, and unwisely, criticized the actions of the army's other two corps. The commanders of those corps, Sherman and James McPherson, exploded with indignation. Sherman labeled the piece "a catalogue of nonsense" that "perverts the Truth to the ends of flattery and Self-glorification; and contains many untruths." Befitting his junior position and restrained personality, McPherson was more formal in his protest to Grant: "The whole tenor of the order is so ungenerous, and the insinuations and criminations against the other Corps of your Army, are so manifestly at variance with the facts, that a sense of duty to my command as well as the verbal protest of every one of my Division and Brigade commanders . . . require that I should call your attention to it." An investigation confirming that McClernand had acted in violation of orders finally gave Grant clear cause to act. "I have found it necessary to relieve Maj. Gen. McClernand," he telegraphed Halleck on June 19, "for his publication of a congratulatory Address calculated to create dissention and ill feeling in the Army. I should have relieved him long since for general unfitness for his position." Did McClernand's writings warrant such a severe penalty as losing his command? By itself alone, probably not; however, McClernand had by this point in the war chronicled a lengthy record of insubordination and political maneuvering that collectively justify Grant's decision. Had Grant not acted when he did, his more competent corps commanders would have rightly questioned his leadership, and, for whatever the war was going to bring in the future, Grant needed them more than he needed McClernand.[35]

The second problem at Vicksburg that had the potential to divert Grant's attention from the task at hand was his predilection for alcohol. Evidently, it resurfaced during the siege in early June, when reports indicated that Joe Johnston's Confederates were on the move near Yazoo City, northeast of Vicksburg. Grant decided to take a steamboat up the Yazoo River to investigate for himself, and it was during this brief journey that one of the most enduring and notorious stories of Grant's drinking was born. There is no question that Grant had difficulty handling spirits, a reputation that began during his posting on the West Coast in the 1850s and that trailed him into the early months of the war, casting a shadow on his character among his superiors, especially Halleck. Grant recognized that he was more susceptible than most to whiskey's ill effects, and in fact John Rawlins, his chief of staff, who was also a trusted friend from his Illinois days, had among his other responsibilities the task of monitoring Grant's headquarters for the presence of alcohol, no small chore in a Civil War camp. Grant himself did what he could to avoid the temptation, as in December 1862 when he reassured his wife, "The bottle of Bourbon sent by Mrs. Davies I sent over to Gen. Sherman. Myself nor no one connected with the Staff ever tasted it." Nevertheless, he occasionally faltered in his self-restraint. The historian Brooks Simpson, whose analysis of the Vicksburg drinking story is one of the more balanced, relates that, while Grant may have had a drink on board the riverboat as it steamed north, the evidence reveals inconsistencies and conflicting "eyewitnesses" that fail to support the contention that Grant was in a stupor that impaired his command abilities. Military rivals and professional jealousy account for many, but certainly not all, of the stories that elevated Grant's wartime drinking to mythic proportions. Charles A. Dana, who had the opportunity to observe Grant on a daily basis throughout most of the war, gave this verdict:

"General Grant's seasons of intoxication were not only infrequent
. . . but he always chose a time when the gratification of his appetite
for drink would not interfere with any important movement that had
to be directed or attended to by him." Like others before and since,
Grant struggled with this plague on his life, but, at Vicksburg and for
the remainder of the war, under the watchful eyes of John Rawlins,
he made sure whiskey remained a personal challenge rather than a
professional problem.[36]

In the meantime, as the warm weather of June turned into the
sweltering heat of a Mississippi July, Federal engineers zigzagged
their approach trenches ever closer to Vicksburg's earthworks. Bak-
ing in rifle pits and redoubts with scant food and diminishing hope,
the Confederates saw they now had little choice but to seek terms of
surrender. On July 3, Pemberton sent word to Grant looking to open
negotiations "to save further effusion of blood," but Grant, holding
to the philosophy he put into practice at Fort Donelson nearly a year
and a half earlier, countered that there was nothing to discuss: "The
useless effusion of blood you propose stopping by this course can
be ended at any time you may choose, by an unconditional surrender of the city and garrison." Despite each man's reluctance to make
concessions, by the end of the day their staff officers had worked out
terms that were agreeable to both, so, on July 4, white flags rose
along the Confederate line; after forty-seven days, the siege of Vicksburg came to an end.[37]

As word of the surrender ran along the lines of blue and gray,
Grant fired off the long-awaited and equally anticipated telegram to
Washington: "The Enemy surrendered this morning. The only terms
allowed is their parole as prisoners of war." Grant had made some
concessions after all, but as he explained to Halleck, "This [the parole
of the Confederates] I regarded as of great advantage to us at this
juncture. It saves probably several days in the capture term—leaves
troops and transports ready for immediate service." By agreeing to
parole the Confederates, meaning that they would be released after
agreeing to stay out of the fight until they were exchanged for an
equivalent number of Federal soldiers under parole, Grant relieved

himself of the responsibility to guard and feed nearly ten thousand men, thereby freeing his own soldiers to continue the war. Initially, he had favored making the Confederates prisoners and shipping them north; however, demonstrating again the flexibility that had become the hallmark of this campaign, he was persuaded by his staff to reconsider. He telegrammed Admiral Porter: "My own feelings are against [parole] but all my officers think the advantage gained by having our forces and transports for immediate purposes more than counterbalance the effect of sending them north." In fact, Grant needed his troops for "immediate purposes" because, even before Vicksburg had surrendered, he had issued new orders setting Sherman's men once again in motion.[38]

Grant intended to keep a tight hold on the initiative by pressing after Joseph E. Johnston's army, which was still loitering in central Mississippi. On July 3, anticipating the imminent occupation of Vicksburg, he sent Sherman a warning order: "When we go in [to Vicksburg], I want you to drive Johnston from the Mississippi Central Rail Road, destroy bridges as far as Granada with your Cavalry and do the enemy all the harm possible." Sherman replied, "If you are in Vicksburg Glory Hallelujah the best fourth of July since 1776." Revealing the degree to which he had come to share his commander's determination to press the Confederates, Sherman confirmed, "Of course we must not rest idle only dont [sic] let us brag too soon. I will order my troops at once to occupy the forks of big black and await with anxiety your further answer." In a note to Grant's chief of staff, Sherman again reiterated his support for immediate action, arguing, "We should follow up rapidly [once Vicksburg is secure] but should leave nothing to chance. Of course we should instantly assume the offensive as against Johnston. . . . Port Hudson is now well invested and an increased force there could do less good than the destruction of the only army that can afford them relief viz Johnston's." When Sherman received word that the surrender of Vicksburg was consummated, he assured Grant, "Already are my orders out to give one big huzza and sling the knapsack for new fields." Grant replied that reinforcements from the other corps were preparing to move out in support and that the objective now was "to drive Johnston out in your own way, and inflict on the enemy all the punishment you can. I will support you to the last man that can be spared." As he had done after the victories at Forts Henry and Donelson, Grant was determined to keep the ball moving and deny his opponent a moment's rest. There would be no celebratory pause; he had the initiative and was committed to pressing his advantage.[39]

The Vicksburg campaign, still a model of operational-level warfare, revealed the extent to which Grant's analytical determination had matured since 1861 and the near battle at Florida, Missouri. For more than eight months, he had had to contend with inclement weather, public criticism, obdurate subordinates, uncooperative superiors, logistical nightmares, the doubts of his most trusted corps commander, and a numerically superior enemy; nevertheless, he had been unwavering in his belief that "a forward movement to a decisive victory was necessary." In overcoming these challenges, the Army of the Tennessee had come to reflect the personality and determination of its commander. Grant's men had trudged through months of mud, cold, and imminent despair, and through those hardships he had won their confidence. "General Grant still retains his hold upon the affections of his men," a reporter wrote in February. "No Napoleonic displays, no ostentation, no speed, no superfluous flummery" kept these men in camp; they stayed because of their commander's "energy and disposition to do something." Despite his earlier skepticism, Sherman acknowledged that Grant had directed "one of the greatest campaigns in history," a military operation that "in its conception and execution belonged exclusively to General Grant, not only in the great whole, but in the thousands of its details." Even General Halleck, ever skeptical of Grant, admitted to Secretary of War Stanton, "We cannot fail to admire the courage and endurance of the troops and the skill and daring of their commander. No more brilliant exploit can be found in military history."[40]

The general's perseverance had also won over his commander-in-chief, something Grant recalled with appreciation after the war:

"With all the pressure brought to bear upon them, both President Lincoln and General Halleck stood by me to the end of the campaign. I had never met Mr. Lincoln, but his support was constant." In early 1863, when the campaign seemed mired in the swamps of Mississippi and Louisiana, Lincoln had dismissed the critics who called for Grant's removal, arguing that he had neither the ability nor the disposition to win. "I think Grant has hardly a friend left, except myself," Lincoln observed. "[But] what I want, and what the people want, is generals who will fight battles and win victories. Grant has done this and I propose to stand by him." When the Vicksburg siege was in its final days, the president again made clear his support: "If Grant only does this thing down there—I don't care much how, so long as he does it *right*—why, Grant is my man and I am his the rest of the war!" Victory, of course, only confirmed the president's faith in this western general who asked for little and produced much. In a sign of his own magnanimity, Lincoln confessed to Grant that had he been in command of the Army of the Tennessee, once Porter's fleet had made its way south of Vicksburg in April, he would have joined Banks in Louisiana. When Grant instead turned away from the river and headed into Mississippi, the president recalled, "I feared it was a mistake. I now wish to make the personal acknowledgement that you were right, and I was wrong."[41]

General Grant's determination was no longer the half-thinking sort that had nearly brought disaster at Shiloh but rather a force of will tempered by confidence and adaptability, derived from experience and reflection. Vicksburg confirmed Grant's status as one of the war's preeminent generals, but the greatest challenge to his leadership and to his will to win was yet to come.

5

Chattanooga

His mind was dwelling upon taking the offensive against the enemy.

—Maj. Horace Porter

The capture of Vicksburg and its garrison was an unmistakable demonstration of Grant's analytical determination and professionalism. From relief to exhaustion, satisfaction to affirmation, the victory undoubtedly evoked a flood of emotions in both the commander and his army. Then for a few glorious days the good news kept coming. On July 4, 1863, the same day of Pemberton's surrender, a telegram arrived from Secretary of War Edwin Stanton notifying Grant of a great victory in the East, where Gen. George Meade had fought a three-day battle against Robert E. Lee at the small Pennsylvania town of Gettysburg. Both sides had suffered untold casualties, but Lee was retreating south, and there was yet hope of his complete destruction. Three days later, on July 7, more good news in another telegram from Washington: the Lincoln administration, fully recognizing the significance of Vicksburg and demonstrating its confidence in Grant, promoted him to major general in the regular army. With the promotion came greater responsibilities, namely, command of the entire western theater of the war, including an increasingly desperate situation at the vital rail center of Chattanooga, Tennessee. First, however, Grant had work to do in Mississippi.[1]

Grant had made clear his determination to pursue Joseph E. Johnston's Rebel force in central Mississippi on July 3, before Vicksburg's final surrender, when he told Sherman to make preparations for offensive operations. The surrender of Port Hudson, Louisiana, on July 9 freed Grant from diverting resources south and allowed him to focus on the enemy in Mississippi. To Sherman he explained that the objective was "to break up Johnstons [*sic*] Army and drive it from our rear, and if possible to destroy the rolling stock, and everything valuable for carrying on War or placing it beyond the reach of the Rebel Army." Sherman understood his commander's intent and was prepared to execute his orders with energy and perseverance. "The wholesale destruction," he wrote on July 14, "to which this country is now being subjected, is terrible to contemplate; but it is the scourge of war, to which ambitious men have appealed rather than the judgment of the learned and pure Tribunals, which our forefathers had provided for supposed wrongs and injuries. Therefore so much of my instructions as contemplated destroying and weakening the resources of our enemy are being executed with rigor, and we have also done much towards the destruction of Johnstons [*sic*] Army." Sherman concluded, "I feel confident of success." Grant encouraged Sherman to "continue the pursuit as long as you have reasonable hopes of favorable results." By July 22, Sherman decided he had reached the point of diminishing returns and called off the pursuit, notifying Grant, "I think we have made a good winding up of the campaign and that the people of Miss are satisfied and want to be let alone on our own terms." The Confederates were not willing to give battle, and Grant had cautioned Sherman not to "wear your men out" on a lengthy chase. Enough was enough.[2]

While Sherman hounded Johnston across the hills of central Mississippi, the Union high command contemplated their next objective. Given that Vicksburg and Port Hudson were now in Federal hands and Johnston's army was on the run, what, Halleck inquired of Grant, "is to be done with the forces available for the field?" Grant replied, "Mobile should be captured." The Alabama port was one of the few places where foreign goods were still seeping their way into the Confederacy and therefore a target of high military value. Grant thought that for logistical reasons his own forces should move on Mobile from New Orleans while additional Federal forces in Missouri moved against Little Rock, Arkansas. Next would come operations against Selma, Alabama. Halleck, who at times seemed to think momentum came in limited quantities and should not be wasted, wanted to put off a move to the Gulf, telling Grant, "Before attempting Mobile, I think it will be best to clean up a little." Grant, irritated by Halleck's demurring, later recalled "that the troops that had done so much should be allowed to do more before the enemy could recover from the blow he had received, and while important points might be captured without bloodshed." Again, Grant drew on his maturing philosophy of war, born on the Fort Donelson campaign, and seasoned on the road to Vicksburg: find your enemy, strike hard, and keep moving; never surrender the initiative. "It seems to me that Mobile is the point deserving the most immediate attention," Grant replied to Halleck. Events elsewhere, however, soon preempted Grant's strategic designs.[3]

While Grant and Halleck debated their next move, Maj. Gen. William S. Rosecrans and the Union Army of the Cumberland were locked in a struggle over middle and eastern Tennessee with the Confederate Army of Tennessee and its contrarian commander, Braxton Bragg. Rosecrans, an 1842 West Point graduate, had butted heads with Grant during the Corinth campaign before ascending to command of the Army of the Cumberland in late October 1862. By late June 1863, he had conducted a near bloodless campaign that forced Bragg to withdraw south into Georgia from Tennessee, leading to the surrender of the vital rail hub of Chattanooga. In early September, Halleck had shifted fifteen regiments of Grant's army from Mississippi to strengthen Rosecrans's hand. The additional manpower, however, was insufficient to stave off a near fatal blow when, on September 19 and 20, Bragg's Rebels narrowly missed an opportunity to destroy the Federals along Chickamauga Creek in northwest Georgia. Only Union general George H. Thomas and his Fourteenth Corps stood firm as Confederates washed over the Federal lines, a performance that earned Thomas the nickname of the "Rock of Chickamauga." The rest of the defeated and dispirited Yankees scurried back to Chattanooga, the army commander, Rosecrans, leading the way.[4]

The defeat rattled the once confident Rosecrans, who now con-

templated pulling back even farther north and allowing Bragg to re-
claim Chattanooga. Fortunately for the Union army, an uninspired
Confederate pursuit allowed Rosecrans to regain his composure and
order the preparation of defensive works. Wars are not won, however,
by defending cities, no matter how important they may be, and at this
moment the defeat at Chickamauga had so debilitated Rosecrans that
he appeared unable to formulate an offensive strategy. Bragg's men
occupied the high ground around Chattanooga, Lookout Mountain
to the south and Missionary Ridge to the east, while a circuitous, narrow, muddy wagon road limited the inflow of Union supplies. The
Army of the Cumberland had become imprisoned in Chattanooga,
and the responsibility fell to its commander to orchestrate a breakout.
But Rosecrans had lost his fighting spirit, and, as he vacillated between resolve and despondency, the army's lack of food was draining
its energy, just as inaction was sapping its morale.[5]

In Washington, administration officials watched with growing dis-
may as a campaign that had once promised the destruction of a Confederate army now teetered on the edge of disaster. New leadership
was needed to supplant the unnerved and demoralized Rosecrans. On
October 16, Grant, in Cairo, Illinois, received a cryptic telegram from
Halleck, ordering him to "immediately proceed to the 'Galt House'
Louisville, Ky, where you will meet an officer of the War Dept with
your orders and instructions." There was an unmistakable sense of
urgency about the message: "You will take with you your staff, etc.,
for immediate operations in the field." Grant set out for Indianapolis
to catch a train to Louisville, but, just as the locomotive was build-
ing steam to pull out of the station, none other than Secretary of
War Edwin Stanton clambered aboard to deliver Grant's new orders.
The president had given the conqueror of Vicksburg command of the
new Military Division of the Mississippi, encompassing a huge swath
of land from the Alleghenies to the Mississippi, from the Ohio River
to the Gulf of Mexico. Tempering Grant's excitement over the new
command, however, was the additional word from Stanton that his
responsibilities included the crisis in Chattanooga, and the implicit
message was clear: save the city and the Army of the Cumberland.[6]

With this command, Grant was at liberty to make a leadership change in the Army of the Cumberland. Rosecrans could remain, or the division commander George Thomas, the hero of Chickamauga, could take over—the choice was Grant's. On October 19, when word came that Rosecrans was contemplating retreat, Grant acted swiftly, firing a telegram to Chattanooga that relieved Rosecrans, elevated Thomas, and ordered him, "Hold Chattanooga at all hazards. I will be there as soon as possible." Even if Rosecrans had not been contemplating a retreat, Grant would have had no difficulty making the command change. The relationship between the two men had soured in the wake of the previous fall's Iuka and Corinth campaign, where, according to Chief of Staff John Rawlins, Grant faulted Rosecrans for a "deviation from the entire plan" by which "the enemy was enabled to escape" and for his "tardiness in pursuit," which allowed Confederate Earl Van Dorn "to get off with much less loss than he should." Grant "could not in justice to himself and the cause of the country think of again commanding General Rosecrans." In Washington, Rosecrans had few friends and fewer defenders, while Grant had the support of Halleck, Stanton, and the president.[7]

George Thomas, a Virginian and West Pointer whose commitment to the Union outweighed any lingering loyalties to his home state, fully understood the gravity of his orders. To Grant's charge to hold the town, Thomas replied exactly as Grant had hoped, in both spirit and substance: "I will hold the town till we Starve." Grant later recalled how much he "appreciated the force of this dispatch," especially once he arrived in the besieged city and saw the enervated state of the Union troops. Reassured by Thomas's resolve, Grant continued on his way to Chattanooga, but before he arrived yet another developing crisis demanded his attention.[8]

At Knoxville, Tennessee, some one hundred miles north of Chattanooga, Gen. Ambrose Burnside and the Army of the Ohio occupied the city, but with a tenuous grip. On October 20, 1863, while still in transit, Grant telegraphed Burnside, "All roads that can be used to get supplies should be put in order as far as possible. . . . Can you not lay in large supplies of forage, bacon, and other supplies by purchase? If so, do it. Have you tools for fortifying? Important points in East Tennessee should be put in condition to be held by the smallest number of men, as soon as possible." At the same time, Grant notified Admiral Porter, who was in Cairo, Illinois, to hurry along the Cumberland River the supplies that would be necessary to sustain Sherman's command, which was making its way east from Mississippi. The desperate situation in eastern Tennessee could have easily overwhelmed Grant, but he was taking the proper steps to gather the available resources. Forces from across the West were now on the move, concentrating in the Chattanooga/Knoxville corridor. New to such a large command, with all its military complications and political implications, Grant demonstrated a sophisticated awareness and comprehension of the strategic and operational situation and relayed to his subordinates his determination to fight for every piece of Union-held territory.[9]

Grant arrived in Chattanooga the evening of October 23, 1863, soaking wet after a grueling mud-slicked trek over the infamous wagon road. At one point, his horse had fallen, aggravating an injury to his left leg. Once in the city, the new commanding officer received a cool welcome from Thomas and his senior officers, who were none too happy to have an outsider taking over their army. Despite his recent promotion to army command, Thomas believed that he had the situation under control and that Grant's assistance was unnecessary. If Grant was put off by the unfriendly reception, his impassiveness revealed no agitation. Pulling a chair up to the fire, he asked the officers for their assessment of the situation, which confirmed earlier reports that nothing else could be done until the troops were getting three meals a day. Grant's thoughts, however, were working well beyond opening a viable supply line, to the primary objective, which was to strike Bragg's army, drive it from the city, and, it was hoped, destroy the Confederates. Horace Porter, a young West Pointer who had served on the staffs of George McClellan and Rosecrans, was one of those gathered around the fireplace. He recalled his first impressions of the western commander: "His questions showed from the outset that his mind was dwelling not only upon the prompt opening of a

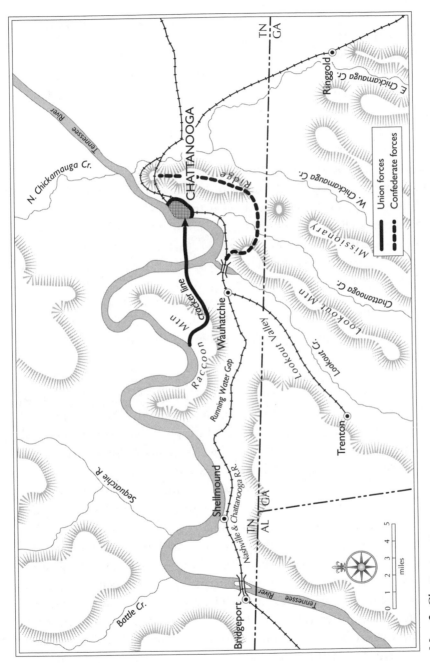

Map 3. Chattanooga

line of supplies, but upon taking the offensive against the enemy. In this he was only manifesting one of his chief military characteristics—an inborn dislike to be thrown upon the defensive."[10]

Offensive operations would come in their own time, but the supply situation demanded immediate attention. Prior to being relieved of command, Rosecrans had designed a plan that involved a pontoon bridge and a minor amphibious assault to open up a shorter and more direct route into Chattanooga. For whatever reason, neither he nor Thomas had been willing to set the operation into motion. Grant reviewed their proposal the night of his arrival and believed it sound. He got the men moving, and soon the "cracker line" was delivering desperately needed goods to the starving army. Giving his subordinates credit, Grant reported to Halleck on October 28, "General Thomas' plan . . . has proven iminently [sic] successful. . . . [T]he question of supplies may now be regarded as settled." The effect on the men was like the raising of Lazarus, Admiral Porter recalled, as "every man now felt that he was no longer to remain on the defensive, but was being supplied and equipped for a forward movement against his old foe."[11]

A debate has since simmered over who deserves the credit for getting the Army of the Cumberland back on its feet: Grant, Thomas, Rosecrans, or even Brig. Gen. William F. "Baldy" Smith, chief engineer of the army. Henry M. Cist, a captain on Rosecrans's staff, acknowledged the contributions of everyone who approved, ordered, and executed the operation, but it was after all "the plan of General Rosecrans." Chief engineer "Baldy" Smith, who was responsible for actually making the plan a reality, credited Grant for getting the ball rolling, "but there is not the slightest reason for doubting that Thomas would have made the same move with the same men and the same results, had General Grant been in Louisville." As for the army commander himself, he praised Thomas for his efforts in crafting the plan, confirming in a telegram to Halleck that Thomas had "set on foot, before my arrival, a plan for geting [sic] possession of the river from a point below Lookout Mountain to Bridgeport." Historians are in agreement that while others had developed the plan conceptually and practically prior to Grant's arrival it took a commander willing to risk failure and exercise his authority in an operation that carried no guarantee of success. The difference between all the other officers involved and Grant was simply—but most significantly—the latter's determination to get the job done, a difference that did not escape one of Grant's staff officers. "It is decisiveness and energy in action," observed John Rawlins, "that always accomplishes grand results, and strikes terror to the heart of the foe, it is this and not the conception of great schemes that make military genius."[12]

Securing a steady flow of wagons alleviated only the most immediate of Grant's concerns. The relative ease with which the Federals opened the cracker line suggested that Bragg, willingly or not, was going to leave the initiative to the Yankees. Grant believed that if the Rebels allowed him one more week of grace "all danger of losing territory now held by us will have passed away, and preparations may commence for offensive opperations [sic]." Of course, there was no way to know for certain what Bragg was planning, and Grant suspected that he might drive for Nashville by striking between Union-held Chattanooga and Knoxville. Realizing that his men would have difficulty blocking such a move, he told Sherman to press forward to Chattanooga as rapidly as possible: "Drop everything east of bear Creek and move with your entire force to Stevenson [Alabama] until you receive further orders. The enemy are evidently moving a large force . . . and may break through our lines." Sherman's report made evident his own determination and how he had come to earn Grant's loyalty and trust: "We work day and night. . . . I will do all that man can to hasten forward." To Burnside in Knoxville, Grant sent instructions that, should the enemy move toward Nashville, "hang on to him with your force," adding that whatever reinforcements could be mustered would be sent from Chattanooga. He was also formulating a plan to make a demonstration against enemy positions around Chattanooga with the expectation of fixing Confederate forces there to forestall an attack elsewhere.[13]

Bragg had indeed been planning a large troop movement, but, instead of an attack toward Nashville, on November 4 he sent Gen.

James Longstreet's corps, temporarily on loan from Lee's Army of Northern Virginia, toward Knoxville in the hopes of taking that city before Grant could shuttle reinforcements to Burnside. From a nervous Washington, both Halleck and Lincoln fretted over Burnside's fate and encouraged Grant to start men toward Knoxville. Grant, however, had no intention of chasing Bragg's wild goose. Recognizing that any detachment sent to Burnside would sufficiently weaken his own force and prevent offensive operations, he developed an alternative that would save Burnside and keep his own army intact. On November 7, he telegraphed his plan to Burnside: "I have ordered an immediate move from here to carry Missionary Ridge. . . . This must have the effect to draw the enemy back from your Western front." In short, attack Bragg at Chattanooga and thereby force him to recall Longstreet. Should Bragg in his turn continue a move toward Knoxville, Grant instructed Burnside to hold key positions but, if overwhelmed, "to fall back . . . into the mountain passes, obstructing the road as you pass." Anticipating imminent battle, he sent orders to expedite the completion of a Nashville to Chattanooga rail line to improve his supply situation. He again encouraged Sherman to move with all possible speed, revealing just how much he had come to rely on this most trusted of subordinates: "The enemy have moved a great part of their force from this front towards Burnside. I have to make an immediate move here toward their lines of communication to bring them back if possible. I am anxious to see your old Corps here at the earliest moment."[14]

Turning to matters close at hand, Grant ordered George Thomas, commanding the Army of the Cumberland there in Chattanooga, to prepare to attack. He impressed on him, "It becomes an imperative duty for your forces to draw the attention of the enemy from Burnside. . . . The movement should not be made one moment later than to-morrow morning." But the following morning, November 8, there was no movement, and there would be none later that day, or for that matter a number of days. Grant's vigorous prodding was not enough to get Thomas, who was at times deliberate to a fault, moving before he was ready. Grant notified Burnside of the delay, encouraging him to hold firm, to which Burnside responded with his intention "to hold in check any force that comes against us until Thomas is ready." Looking for alternatives to relieve the pressure on Burnside, Grant issued orders to his cavalry to move out: "Where an enemy makes his appearance . . . never wait orders to pursue, but . . . start at once simply reporting what they are doing." By November 14, the situation at Knoxville had become desperate. A telegram from a jittery Halleck revealed, "Burnside was hesitating whether to fight or retreat. I fear he will not fight, although strongly urged to do so. Unless you can give him immediate assistance, he will surrender his position." Grant assured Halleck, "I am pushing everything to give Gen. Burnside early aid. I have impressed on him in the strongest terms the necessity of holding on to his position." And indeed Grant had; two days before his exchange with Halleck, he had warned Burnside, "It is of the most vital importance that East Tennessee should be held: Take immediate steps to that end." And even more forcefully the following day: "I do not know how to impress on you the necessity of holding on to East Tennessee, in strong enough terms. . . . I can hardly conceive the necessity of retreating from East Tennessee. If I did so at all it would be after losing most of the Army." As events played out, such a sacrifice would prove unnecessary. Halleck's and Grant's urgings steeled Burnside, and Longstreet's Confederates never seriously threatened the Union hold on Knoxville. Even when the loss of East Tennessee seemed imminent, Grant confided to his wife that he remained confident of success, both there at Chattanooga and in the larger war effort. "I am very hopeful and fully believe," he wrote on November 14, "if not failed by any officer in immediate command, that all will show the Union forces in a more favorable position twenty days hence than they have been in since the begining [sic] of the rebelion [sic]." His prediction would prove accurate, but, more significant, his quiet confidence during one of the darker moments of the Chattanooga campaign again reveals an optimism and determination that had become the hallmark of his leadership and were increasingly shared by the soldiers he led.[15]

The threat to Knoxville had not distracted Grant from his objective of seizing the initiative and driving Bragg's force away from Chattanooga. Rain had slowed the long-anticipated arrival of Sherman's Army of the Tennessee, forcing Grant to postpone an attack he had planned for November 21, eliciting a rare display of frustration in a telegram to Halleck: "I have never felt such restlessness before as I have at the fixed and immovable condition of the Army of the Cumberland." On November 23, when signs again indicated that Confederate forces might be heading north toward Knoxville, Grant decided he could await Sherman no longer. Demonstrating the battlefield flexibility that had characterized the Vicksburg campaign, he ordered Thomas to advance his forces toward Missionary Ridge to a piece of high ground known as Orchard Knob, with the limited objective of capturing enemy outposts. If the Federals could not execute an all-out attack, they could at least put on a demonstration that would pull Bragg's attention back from Knoxville. That afternoon, Thomas's men stepped off with parade ground precision and pushed back Rebel pickets, seizing Orchard Knob. More important, the attack accomplished its primary objective of forcing Bragg to recall the two divisions he had set on the road to Knoxville. In the meantime, Grant sent word to Sherman's lead division, pressing them to come up as quickly as possible: "You must get up with your force tomorrow without fail. Pass the wagon train and leave it to follow your rear guard. If you cannot get up with your Artillery, come without it, leaving it to follow." That evening, Sherman finally arrived and, concurring with Grant, stated, "No cause on earth will induce me to ask for longer delay. . . . Every military reason now sanctions a general attack. Longstreet is absent, and we expect no more re-enforcements, therefore we should not delay another hour, and should put all our strength in the attack." One can only imagine Grant's relief and satisfaction. He was finally reunited with the man who most understood and shared his approach to war, and both were determined to strike and strike hard.[16]

Just after his arrival in Chattanooga, Grant had assured Halleck of his intention "to get the troops in a state of readiness for a forward movement at the earliest [sic] possible day." On November 24, that day had finally come. Grant's plan was simple enough—attack both flanks of Bragg's army in anticipation of finding a weakness. Sherman's westerners would cross the Cumberland River north of Chattanooga to attack Confederate positions on the northern end of Missionary Ridge while Joe Hooker's Army of the Potomac boys advanced against the southern anchor of the Rebel line at Lookout Mountain; Thomas's Army of the Cumberland would stand by in the center as a reserve. Relieving some of Grant's long-festering frustration, the day's attacks began on time despite a cold rain, and, although by the end of the day neither Sherman nor Hooker had achieved a breakthrough, they had made progress, and Grant was optimistic that the morrow would prove decisive.[17]

The rain had cleared by the next morning, and from his headquarters on the prominence of Orchard Knob, "where a plan could be followed and from one place the whole field be within one view," the commander looked to his generals to renew their attacks. Grant appeared a study of quiet, sober confidence, the lessons of Florida, Missouri, again at play. Difficult terrain and tenacious Rebels on both flanks slowed early progress, and by midday the assaults had bogged down. The smoke erupting from Grant's cigar signaled the return of earlier frustrations. Sensing that the battle's decisive moment was at hand, Grant ordered Thomas to advance the Fourth and Fourteenth Corps against the base of Missionary Ridge, looking to draw Confederates away from the flanks. Minutes passed with no movement of Thomas's men. Grant again instructed Thomas to have his men move out against the Confederate rifle pits dotting the bottom of the ridge. Once more, minutes came and went without a single regiment moving forward. Enough of military propriety and the chain of command; Grant bypassed Thomas, who in truth opposed the assault, and his corps commanders. Going directly to Brig. Gen. Thomas Wood, in charge of one of the divisions responsible for the attack, Grant asked him "why he did not charge as ordered an hour before. He replied very promptly that this was the first he had heard of it. . . . I told him to make the charge at once. He was off in a moment, and in an incredibly short time loud cheering was heard." The advancing Federals sent Rebel pickets scampering up the ridge as they washed over the Confederate outposts and began to sweep up the slope. This last movement surprised everyone, including Grant, since he had issued no orders to take the ridge. Brig. Gen. Joseph S. Fullerton, a staff officer present on Orchard Knob, recalled that Grant, furious at yet another apparent disregard for his wishes, turned on Thomas first, demanding, "Who ordered those men up the ridge?" When Thomas denied culpability, Grant's gaze locked on Fourth Corps commander Gordon Granger, who was equally surprised at the uphill charge but offered as a possible explanation, "When those fellows get started all hell can't stop them." Finding no one to blame, Grant turned back to watch the ongoing assault and in doing so witnessed one of the most astounding feats of the war. The long-beleaguered and -belittled men of the Army of the Cumberland who had suffered through the siege of Chattanooga at last came of age, carrying the heights of Missionary Ridge, and driving the southerners from their earthworks, nearly captured Braxton Bragg himself.[18]

Seeing that momentum had suddenly swung his way, Grant moved quickly to press the advantage, signaling Sherman on the Confederates' right flank, "Thomas has carried the hill and line in his immediate front. Now is your time to attack with vigor. DO SO!" But further action from Sherman proved unnecessary as Bragg's line was in shards and his men were in rapid retreat to the south. Still, Grant was unwilling to let his foe escape without inflicting as much damage as possible. As the sun set on what had been a grand day for the Federals, orders went out to General Thomas, "Start a strong reconnoisance [*sic*] in the morning at 7 A.M. to ascertain the position of the enemy. If it is ascertained that the enemy are in full retreat, follow them with all your force." "I think we will push Bragg with all our strength to-morrow," Grant informed Sherman that same evening, "and try if we cannot cut off a good portion of his rear troops and trains. His men have manifested a strong disposition to desert for some time past and we will now give them a chance." The bluecoats pursued the Rebels for the next three days, driving them beyond Ringgold, Georgia, where Grant gave up the chase to turn his attention back north to the culminating crisis in Knoxville.[19]

Even as the last Confederates were pulling back from the heights of Missionary Ridge on November 25, Grant's first thoughts were on getting help to Union forces in East Tennessee: "The next thing now will be to relieve Burnside." General Granger's Fourth Corps set out for Knoxville within forty-eight hours, but his advance was too slow for Grant, who on November 29 prodded him with a reminder of what was at stake: "I want to urge upon you in the strongest possible manner, the necessity of reaching Burnside in the shortest possible time. Our victory here has been complete, and if Longstreet can be driven from E. Tennessee, the damage to the Confederacy will be the most crushing they have experienced during the war." Despite this encouragement, Grant believed Granger had already "decided for himself that it was a very bad move to make," so that same day he signaled Sherman, "Granger is on the way to Burnside's relief but I have lost all faith in his energy or capacity to manage an expedition of the importance of this one. . . . In plain words you will assume command of all the forces now moving up the Tennessee [River] . . . and from that force organize what you deem proper to relieve Burnside." To Burnside, Grant sent word that reinforcements were on the way and "to hold to the very last moment," which in the end Burnside did, beating back a final, desperate Confederate assault on November 29, and forcing Longstreet to give up his siege of Knoxville on December 3. Ten days of bitter fighting and forced marches had secured for Grant and his Federals firm and final control of Chattanooga and eastern Tennessee.[20]

With the Rebels driven from Tennessee into Georgia and Knoxville securely in Union hands, standard procedure would have been to settle into winter quarters. This would allow the army to recover and refit from its weeks of campaigning and, especially in this instance, give its commander the opportunity to enjoy the praise and notoriety for having won yet another victory. But, as was his practice following Fort Donelson, Shiloh, and Vicksburg, Grant was committed to pressing the initiative, winter weather or not. "I do not feel satisfied," he told James McPherson, "giving the rebels so much time for reorganizing, nor in keeping so large a force idle." So he proposed to

Halleck an expedition to Mobile, Alabama, as he had done after the Vicksburg campaign and before the crisis at Chattanooga. Watching the events in Tennessee with mounting anxiety, Robert E. Lee was concerned enough to warn Jefferson Davis that "as large a force as possible" should be sent to "insure [*sic*] the discomfiture of Grant's army. Upon the defense of the country threatened by General Grant depends the safety of the points now held by us on the Atlantic." Confederate general P. G. T. Beauregard concurred, recommending the concentration of "every soldier possible for operations against General Grant." The Confederate commanders, however, could see the threat Grant posed more clearly than General Halleck, who, true to form, was hesitant to rush ahead and instead instructed Grant to secure ground already gained, especially East Tennessee since Longstreet's southerners were still milling about. Bowing to the general-in-chief's recommendations, Grant again set aside his aspirations for Mobile and sent a cavalry force to shadow Longstreet. After the first of the year, he returned Sherman to Vicksburg to lead what would become the Meridian Expedition. From Chattanooga, Thomas would carry out a demonstration toward Atlanta to keep the Confederates confused and their forces divided. Halleck contemplated no significant follow-up to the Chattanooga campaign's conclusion. Grant had now endured Halleck's equivocations for nearly two years, but, unknown to him, steps were being taken to make him answerable to one man only, that being the president. News of a change in the Union command structure would reach the victor of Chattanooga in time to map out a comprehensive Union strategy for the upcoming 1864 campaign.[21]

Grant's successful Vicksburg campaign in July 1863 had won him increased respect and furthered President Lincoln's support; it also led to command of the Military Division of the Mississippi, which encompassed the western theater of war and three separate armies. Military history offers up more than a few examples of men promoted beyond their abilities, and the Civil War is no exception; Richard Ewell's elevation from division to corps command in Lee's Army of Northern Virginia comes to mind, along with most of the commanders of the Union Army of the Potomac. With the Chattanooga campaign, Grant disproved his longtime critics, who had always presumed that he was a bumbler and a drunkard, a man carried for so long by luck that surely the next promotion would expose his supreme incompetence. From July to December 1863, he demonstrated the operational and tactical skills necessary to win at the level of a modern-day army group commander. Directly related, he continued to exercise analytical determination and instill in his subordinates a commitment to victory.

As he had done during the Vicksburg campaign, while operating in East Tennessee Grant adapted to the changing battlefield environment while keeping his sights on the ultimate objective, to take the offensive and drive the Confederates from Chattanooga. Operationally, within hours of his arrival in Chattanooga, he set to solving the army's supply crisis by executing the cracker line plan. Then, on November 23, with the situation a hundred miles away in Knoxville reaching its culminating point, Grant exercised tactical flexibility by forgoing Sherman's planned attack at Chattanooga and instead ordering a demonstration by Thomas that captured Orchard Knob and froze Longstreet's men in place. Two days later, he again sent Thomas's command forward toward Missionary Ridge when the anticipated flank attacks of Sherman and Hooker faltered. In each instance, Grant had developed a plan and then with continuous evaluation of the developing battle adapted to events.[22]

The months of October and November confirmed that Lincoln and Stanton had made a wise decision to promote Grant to the equivalent of theater command. Unlike after Vicksburg, Lincoln had no confessions of misjudgment to make when he signaled Grant on December 8, effusive with praise: "Understanding that your lodgment at Chattanooga and Knoxville is now secure, I wish to tender you, and all under your command, my more than thanks—my profoundest gratitude—for the skill, courage, and perseverance, with which you and they, over so great difficulties, have effected that important object. May God bless you all." Grant's analytical and organizational

capabilities, coupled with his clarity of mind in identifying and pri-
oritizing multiple objectives, kept independent forces all working
toward the primary mission of securing eastern Tennessee. Some
might argue that, at Chattanooga as at Vicksburg, Grant did not face
the Confederacy's best commanders. It is certainly true that Bragg
headed up a dysfunctional collection of insubordinate and uncooperative generals. Grant himself acknowledged that at Chattanooga he
had received help from the most unlikely of sources, the Confederate
president. "Mr. Davis had an exalted opinion of his own military genius," Grant wrote in reference to the decision to shift James Longstreet's men away from Chattanooga toward Knoxville. "On several
occasions during the war he came to the relief of the Union army by
means of his *superior military genius.*" Sarcasm aside, Grant showed
the skill and determination to extract the Army of the Cumberland
from a precarious situation that had paralyzed its previous commanders. Time would give him the opportunity to test himself against the
South's best generals, but for the moment he had defeated every
leader the Confederacy had thrown at him.[23]

The final point in this assessment of Grant's leadership in the
Chattanooga campaign focuses on his relationships with his subordinates and superiors. His quiet and unassuming approach to overcoming obstacles and pressing on to victory continued to win over the
officers serving in his command. Gen. O. O. Howard, commander of
the Army of the Potomac's Eleventh Corps, which joined the fight
at Chattanooga, described the situation there as "completely 'out of
joint' when we first arrived. A *most complete and perfect want* of system prevailed, from Louisville to Chattanooga. I can now feel the
difference. . . . I cannot be too thankful for the policy that placed
these three Depts. under Grant." Col. L. B. Eaton echoed Howard's
thoughts, writing, "You have no conception of the change in the
army when Grant came. He opened up the cracker line and got a
steamer through. We began to see things move. We felt that everything came from a plan. He came into the army quietly, no splendor,
no airs, no staff. He used to go about alone. He began the campaign
the moment he reached the field." Grant's relationship with the most

important and valuable of his subordinates, William T. Sherman, matured during this campaign into the most effective military partnership of the war. The newspaperman Sylvanus Cadwallader witnessed most of the battle in close proximity to Grant, including those moments when Sherman's attack stumbled on the northern end of Missionary Ridge. "That's where Sherman is posted; he'll soon make it all right," was Grant's "quiet, self-assured" comment to Cadwallader. This impressed on the reporter that "Grant's confidence in Sherman had come to be unbounded. Under given conditions he knew precisely how far he could depend on him. . . . His temporary repulses never caused a moment's uneasiness, or doubt as to his final success." Sherman possessed an equally limitless faith in Grant, assuring him after the campaign, "You occupy a position of more power than Halleck or the President. . . . Your reputation as a general is now far above that of any man living." The trusted friend then offered some well-founded advice: "Do as you have heretofore done. Preserve a plain military character, and let others maneuver as they will. You will beat them not only in fame, but in doing good in the closing scenes of this war." In Sherman, Grant had found a general who shared his philosophy of war and an unrelenting commitment to success and a friend in whom he could place his full trust.[24]

Unlike Sherman, others in the officer corps still remained skeptical of Grant's abilities despite, or perhaps because of, his ever-growing record of significant victories. George Thomas's chilly reception on Grant's arrival in Chattanooga boded ill for their future interaction, a harbinger that proved accurate, if not necessarily self-fulfilling. The obstinacy—some might say outright refusal—that Thomas displayed in carrying out Grant's orders on Orchard Knob severely strained their ability to work together. As Cadwallader believed, it was "the beginning of Grant's comparative lack of confidence in Gen. Thomas." Grant knew Thomas was a good soldier when fighting on defense but feared "that when he was left to act on his own responsibility he would be too slow in assuming the offensive." The "Rock of Chickamauga" lacked the quality that distinguished the great general from the good, that quality that Sherman and Grant exercised to powerful effect, an unremitting will to seize and maintain the offensive in pursuit of victory.[25]

Maj. Gen. Joe Hooker, who commanded the two corps of the Army of the Potomac that participated in the Chattanooga fight, was another subordinate who was less than enamored with Grant's decisionmaking. Specifically, he questioned Grant's order to call off the pursuit of Bragg in the days immediately after the battle. "The great mistake of all," Hooker informed Secretary of War Stanton in February 1864, "was in checking the pursuit at Ringgold, [Georgia,] for if one-half of the marching had been done there that was done in going to Knoxville[,] the greater part of Bragg's army, and certainly all of its material, would now have been ours." His criticism of Grant, however, must have stemmed from either a lack of strategic knowledge or a failure to appropriately prioritize objectives. Grant commented on the decision to halt the pursuit in his report on the battle submitted in late December 1863, explaining, "Had it not been for the imperative necessity of relieving Burnside I would have pursued the broken and demoralized retreating enemy. . . . But my advices were that Burnside's supplies would only last until about the 3rd of December. . . . I determined therefore to pursue no further." Grant's "advices" came from his superior, General-in-Chief Halleck, who on November 23, at the same moment Thomas's men were moving to take Orchard Knob, cabled Grant, "I fear that Genl Burnside is hard pressed, and that any further delay may prove fatal." Two days later, Lincoln weighed in, brief but clear: "Remember Burnside." Even if Grant believed that after the battle Bragg should have been the most immediate military objective, he understood that war, as Clausewitz makes clear, is at its most fundamental a political undertaking and that the president, not the generals, has the responsibility and the authority to make decisions of national strategy. He accepted that in a democracy military commanders must be prepared to adapt to the demands of their civilian leaders.[26]

By this point in the war, a number of men, some of whom were initially ill disposed toward Grant, had had the opportunity to observe him in close proximity, and from them a consensus emerges as to the kind of leader Grant had become. Charles Francis Adams, grandson of John Adams, son of John Quincy, and during the war U.S. ambassador to Great Britain, described the general as "cool and quiet . . . and in a crisis he is one against whom all around, whether few in numbers or a great army as here, would instinctively lean," the very definition of Clausewitz's great force of will. Assistant Secretary of War Charles A. Dana, sent by the secretary of war to monitor Grant's headquarters because of lingering doubts about his fitness for command, wrote, "He is the most modest, the most disinterested, and the most honest man I have ever known." Maj. Gen. David Hunter, another observer from Washington, echoed Dana's assessment and identified in Grant the analytical abilities that distinguish determination from stubbornness: "He is a hard worker, writes his own dispatches and orders, and does his own thinking. . . . He listens quietly to the opinions of others and then judges promptly for himself; and he is very prompt to avail himself in the field of all the errors of his enemy." John A. Rawlins, Grant's close friend and chief of staff, summed up his commander's philosophy and deceptively simple formula for winning: "Harmonise [*sic*] all into *one purpose namely the defeat of the enemy.* . . . Unostentatious in his manners[,] ambitious only for his country's success, he . . . wins success where others fail, in the field."[27]

With Chattanooga now secure, another promotion was in the offing. It would carry Grant to the heights of the army and his profession, but it would also bring greater responsibility. He was about to face his most difficult challenges of the war, designing and executing an overarching strategy for the Union war effort, and facing the Confederacy's best general, Robert E. Lee.

6

The Overland Campaign

There is no fall back with U. S. Grant.
　　　　　　　　　　　　　　—A New York soldier

By January 1864, the nation had endured two and a half years of a tragic civil war, including some of the most traumatic political, economic, and social convulsions the country had ever witnessed. These disruptions paled in comparison to the loss of life and the physical and emotional wounds inflicted on both soldier and civilian, and no honest person could look ahead and see the nightmare's end. For those charged with prosecuting the war, there was no respite, and, as far as Ulysses S. Grant was concerned, the quickest, if not the only, way to end the war was to fight—fight today, fight tomorrow, and tomorrow again, until the Confederates had no fight left. Grant's commitment to the relentless pursuit and destruction of the enemy would reach its zenith in 1864, a year that began with the momentum in the Union camp, thanks to the victory at Chattanooga.

Despite having his plans for an immediate drive on Mobile thwarted by Halleck's caution, in January Grant informed George Thomas that, "at the earliest possible moment in the Spring," his Army of the Cumberland would strike out from Chattanooga for Mobile by going through Atlanta, then Montgomery, Alabama. But the first matter of business was taking care of Longstreet's force, which remained in East Tennessee. "Old Pete's" Confederates were more of a nuisance than a real threat, but their presence could disrupt Grant's campaign plans. Moreover, Halleck wanted Longstreet driven out of Tennessee and into Virginia, so Grant set part of his army moving, sending off Maj. Gen. John Schofield's men. "I deem it of the utmost importance to drive Longstreet out immediately," he telegraphed Schofield, "so as . . . to prepare for a Spring Campaign of our own choosing instead of permitting the enemy to dictate it for us." To Brig. Gen. Alvin P. Hovey, who was organizing new troops in Indianapolis, Grant shared his expectation that "we will have some sharp fighting in the spring, and if successful, I believe the war will be ended within the year; if the enemy gain temporary advantage, the war will be protracted." Implicit in both messages was Grant's determination to maintain the initiative when the war resumed in earnest that spring.[1]

Grant's focus and drive in the West were in sharp contrast to the Federals' situation in Washington, where dissatisfaction and impatience were growing with the Army of the Potomac and General-in-Chief Halleck. Brig. Gen. James H. Wilson, an engineering officer and member of Grant's staff, advised his commander in early February, "No hope is entertained that the Army of the Potomac can or will do much. It *must* be regenerated." President Lincoln expressed similar concerns about Halleck's lethargic prosecution of the war, recalling that Halleck had demanded full control over all military assets on taking command but that, since the Union's drubbing by Lee at Second Bull Run in August 1862, the general-in-chief had "shrunk from responsibility whenever it was possible." Once again, Lincoln concluded that a change in command must be made, and this time he believed he had found the right man for the job.[2]

On February 26, 1864, the House of Representatives and the Senate passed a bill reviving the rank of lieutenant general, and three days later the president nominated Ulysses S. Grant for the post. On March 2, the Senate confirmed the promotion, making Grant the first man to hold that rank since George Washington. The next day, Grant received orders to report immediately to Washington, where on March 9 at the White House he received his commission from Lincoln, who in congratulating Grant reminded him that "with this high honor devolves upon you also, a corresponding responsibility," the challenges of which the new lieutenant general was all too well aware. Grant was now the highest ranking officer in the Union army and, therefore, would replace Halleck as general-in-chief, take com-

mand of all Federal forces, and assume responsibility for a comprehensive war strategy. Halleck would remain in Washington acting as
chief of staff, but the war was now Grant's to win or lose.[3]

After the commissioning ceremony, the president and his new
commander huddled together to discuss war philosophy and strategy,
each relieved and reassured to find the other a man with whom he
could work. According to Grant, Lincoln all but confessed a complete lack of military expertise but underscored that as president he
had to consider factors other than military in prosecuting the war.
Most significant among them was maintaining public and congressional support. There would come a time, Lincoln warned, when "the
spirits and resources of the people would become exhausted." The
failure of previous commanders to grasp this political reality of a democracy at war had led Lincoln to issue a series of "'executive orders'
principally for the purpose of hurrying the movement of commanding generals." In Grant, however, he believed he had a military man
who "knew the value of minutes" and understood that wars were
fought as much on election day and in the halls of governance as on
the battlefield. Comforted and encouraged by a newfound optimism,
Lincoln assured Grant that "he was not going to interfere" in military
operations.[4]

When Grant begged off a dinner invitation from the president so
he could return to the front, Lincoln knew his assessment of Grant
was spot on. Shortly after Grant's departure, the president shared
his impressions of the general with one of his secretaries, William O.
Stoddard. The new general-in-chief, Lincoln mused, was "the quiet-
est little fellow you ever saw. . . . The only evidence you have that
he's in any place is that he makes things git! Wherever he is, things
move." Then, poking a finger at his secretary, Lincoln exclaimed,
"[Grant is] the first general I've had. He's a general. . . . You know
how it's been with all the rest. As soon as I put a man in command
of the army, he'd come to me with a plan of campaign and about as
much say, 'Now, I don't believe I can do it, but if you say so, I'll try
it on,' and so put the responsibility of success or failure on me. They
all wanted me to be the general. It isn't so with Grant. He hasn't told

me what his plans are. I don't know, and I don't want to know. I'm glad to find a man who can go ahead without me." For now, Grant had the president's confidence, but he had yet to demonstrate that he could effectively command at the highest level; moreover, he had yet to prove, as Stoddard, Lincoln's secretary, pointed out to the president, "that he can handle the Army of the Potomac and beat Lee on his own ground." Time would tell if President Lincoln's faith was warranted.[5]

Having succeeded Grant in command of the Military District of Mississippi, Sherman wrote from Memphis reveling in Grant's promotion, styling him as "Washington's legitimate successor." Effusive with praise, Sherman put his finger on the reason for Grant's continued and consistent success: "The chief characteristic in your nature is the simple faith in success you have always manifested. . . . This faith gave you victory at Shiloh and Vicksburg. Also when you have completed your best preparations you go into Battle without hesitation, as at Chattanooga—no doubts—no reserve, and I tell you that it was this that made us act with confidence." This latter point reveals how Grant's confidence and determination had transformed many of those under his command. Sherman, who in 1861 had suffered the ignominy of being relieved of command for alleged mental instability, had now served with Grant for over two years and risen to command all Federal forces in the western theater of war, which he would do with Grant-like resolve and drive. He also warned Grant of the insidious dangers lurking in the nation's capital, reminding him that other generals had been overwhelmed by the assaults of bureaucrats and politicians. "For God's sake and for your Country's," Sherman pleaded, "come out of Washington . . . come out West," predicting that together they would finish the job for which so many had already sacrificed so much.[6]

Grant was in accord with his lieutenant's thinking and initially planned on making his headquarters in the familiar West, but, after traveling to the capital and meeting with the president, he acknowledged that he could not effectively direct the war from such a distance. He knew his place as commanding general had to be in

Washington, or at least in the East, but Sherman need not have feared for Grant in the tar pit of Washington politics. The new general-in-chief would keep his headquarters where it had always been, in the field with the army.[7]

Nearly three years earlier, while posted in Cairo, Illinois, Grant had dreamed of one day commanding a cavalry brigade in the Army of the Potomac, which had been the Union's glamour army in the early months of the war. By August 1863, a more experienced and politically savvy Grant confided to Charles A. Dana that he had no interest in taking command of that army. In the West, he knew the roads and rivers, he knew which officers he could rely on and which ones had to be watched, and he knew that his soldiers had come to rely on and trust him. To be ordered east, Grant confessed, "would cause me more sadness than satisfaction." Given the Army of the Potomac's frequent drubbings at the hands of Lee and its roster of dysfunctional generals, who in the summer of 1863 could blame Grant for being less than enthusiastic about such a prospect? Eight months later, the newly promoted Grant found himself in command of that army, but little else had changed. As had always been the case, it was the Union's largest and best-equipped force, but, unlike Grant's old command, the Army of the Tennessee, the Army of the Potomac lacked confidence. There was pomp and pageantry but little of the cocksure swagger of Grant's westerners.[8]

Maj. Gen. George Gordon Meade, a professional soldier with a reputation for competent, if uninspired, generalship, had led the Army of the Potomac since June 28, 1863. He had succeeded Joe Hooker just three days before the Battle of Gettysburg, where he won recognition and the public's gratitude for defeating Lee during those three bloody days in July. Yet his failure to pursue and destroy the Rebels in the battle's aftermath so disappointed Lincoln that the president despaired of ever beating the Confederates. "Great God!" the president sighed when word came that Lee was slipping away across the Potomac, "What does it mean? . . . Our Army held the war in the hollow of their hand and they would not close it." With Grant's promotion and arrival in the East nine months later, Meade began mentally packing his bags, but, after a meeting between the two, Grant chose to keep Meade in place. He recognized that Meade was an efficient army administrator, knew the officer corps and the local geography, and, most important, was all business, a man with whom Grant could work. For the time being at least, Meade would continue to command the Army of the Potomac as if Grant was in a Washington office, rather than a tent just a few paces away.[9]

For his part, Grant was pleased by the condition of the army, a reflection of Meade's administrative skills. The army, he wrote in April, "is in splendid condition and evidently feel [*sic*] like whipping somebody. I feel much better with this command than I did before seeing it." Not everyone in the officer corps, however, shared their new commander's optimism. Among them was Col. Charles S. Wainwright, the Fifth Corps' chief of artillery, who having known Grant before the war found it difficult to think of him as "a great man," given his reputation for "the mediocrity of his mind" and "his insatiable love of whiskey." As for the rank and file, Wainwright saw "no enthusiasm shown by the men on the arrival of their new commander," who reviewed the troops "in a slouchy unobservant way, with his coat unbuttoned and setting anything but an example of military bearing to the troops." Others undoubtedly shared Wainwright's tepid reaction to General Grant, but some saw in this diminutive "little fellow" something more than a shabby soldier who had enjoyed an extraordinary run of good luck. An officer on Meade's staff observed that "Grant wears an expression as if he had determined to drive his head through a brick wall and was about to do it," a sentiment shared by a Wisconsin veteran who observed, "He looks as if he meant it," and by a New Englander who with guarded hope remarked, "We all felt at last that *the boss* had arrived." More than likely, most soldiers, both officers and enlisted, held the attitude of a Second Corps officer who was neither put off by Grant's appearance or prewar reputation nor won over by his success in the West. What mattered was the present, and the accolades would come in due course, "when he shows himself the great soldier here in Virginia against Lee and the best troops of the Rebels."[10]

Defeating Lee and his Rebel army was the primary reason Lincoln had brought Grant east, and on taking command Grant began planning to do just that. In January 1864, prior to his promotion and at Henry Halleck's request, Grant had submitted a plan to force Lee out of Virginia by cutting his supply line at Raleigh, North Carolina, and, while the proposal went no further than Halleck's desk, it showed that Grant was already thinking in terms of national strategy. Strategic thinking had been a point of contention between Lincoln and his top commanders since early in the war. In an 1862 letter to Gen. Don Carlos Buell, the president outlined a broad strategy that he believed took advantage of the Federals' preponderance of resources to stretch the Confederates' inferior manpower to the breaking point. "We have the *greater* numbers," the president wrote on January 13, 1862, "and the enemy has the *greater* facility of concentrating forces upon points of collision; that we must fail, unless we can find some way of making *our* advantage an overmatch for *his;* and that this can only be done by menacing him with superior forces at *different* points, at the *same* time." To counter the Confederate advantage of interior lines, Lincoln was proposing that the Union could best use its numerical advantage by launching multiple, simultaneous offensives. Beginning with McClellan, Union commanders roundly dismissed the president's thinking as the flights of an uninformed amateur. One can therefore imagine Lincoln's satisfaction and sense of vindication when he discovered Grant not only understood but planned to implement just such a strategy. As Grant saw it, the primary shortcoming in the Union's previous strategies was that "the armies had acted separately and independently of each other, giving the enemy an opportunity often of depleting one command, not pressed, to reinforce another more actively engaged. I determined to stop this." Rather than leaving soldiers in static defenses that did nothing to advance the war, Grant wanted coordinated forward movement across all fronts. Lincoln summed up Grant's strategy for simultaneous offensives as only a country lawyer could: "If a man can't skin he must hold a leg while somebody else does."[11]

With the president's support, Grant set about gathering all the maps and reports of unit strength he could get his hands on and fore-warned his senior officers that he wanted "all troops in the field that can be got for the Spring Campaign." Grant's desire to get the maxi-mum number of men actively engaged in the war touched off his first confrontation with a Washington bureaucrat, Secretary of War Edwin Stanton, who protested that the troop redeployments left the capital vulnerable to Rebel attack. In a demonstration of his self-confidence and comfort with his rank, Lt. Gen. Grant informed Stanton, "I think I rank you in the matter, Mr. Secretary." Stanton, a man who enjoyed his own share of self-confidence, turned to the president to settle the matter, which Lincoln did, in favor of his general-in-chief.[12]

The manpower question being settled, Grant developed his strat-egy for the coming campaign, a five-part assault on the Confederacy consisting of three minor operations, those "holding a leg," and two major offensives, which would do the "skinning." For the secondary offensives, Maj. Gen. Nathaniel Banks would lead an attack against Mobile, Alabama; Maj. Gen. Franz Sigel was to move a force south into the Shenandoah Valley to fix enemy forces and prevent their movement to other theaters; and Maj. Gen. Benjamin Butler would land an army on the Virginia coast and advance along the James Riv-er toward Richmond. In addition to detailing specific campaign or-ders, Grant reminded each commander that coordinated movement among the Union offensives was imperative and that each was to do his utmost to achieve success. In truth, Grant had little hope that any of these secondary expeditions would produce a significant victory, or much of a victory at all for that matter, for each commander was a political appointee whose generalship fell somewhere between medi-ocre and inept. Nevertheless, any action on their part would consume scarce Confederate resources and deny their use elsewhere.[13]

Grant's low expectations for these three operations were bal-anced by his absolute faith in the eventual success of the two main of-fensives. William Tecumseh Sherman would drive from Chattanooga toward Atlanta, and Grant's own campaign, spearheaded by George Meade and the Army of the Potomac, would move against Lee and the battle-tested veterans of the Army of Northern Virginia. In early

April, Grant laid out his overarching strategy for Sherman, including marching orders "to move against [Joseph E.] Johnston's Army, to break it up and to get into the interior of the enemy's country as far as you can, inflicting all the damage you can against their War resources." It was understood that Sherman would advance from Chattanooga to Atlanta, but beyond that Grant was willing to leave the details to his most trusted subordinate. Sherman acknowledged the orders, asking only to be told the moment the campaign was to begin to ensure "simultaneous action" across "the Grand Theatre of War." A few days later, a note from Sherman reaffirmed Grant's faith: "I will not let side issues draw me off from your main plans in which I am to knock Jos. Johnston." This was a nice summary of Grant's own approach to war and reflective of one of the most important lessons from the Vicksburg campaign, indeed, if not all Grant's campaigns—keep your eye on the ultimate objective.[14]

Grant had no qualms about giving Sherman complete latitude in the conduct of the Atlanta campaign, but he did not have the same confidence in George Meade, despite the latter's solid, if not spectacular, record. In the Virginia theater, Grant wanted the reigns in his hands as he set out to battle Lee. Meade would in fact continue to command the Army of the Potomac, but Grant's immediate presence would keep the campaign moving toward its objective, Lee's Army of Northern Virginia. Previous commanders had made their target the Confederate capital of Richmond, and each commander in turn gave up his efforts after a sound whipping administered by Lee. Beginning in the spring of 1864, however, a new Federal strategy began to take form in the correspondence between Grant and Halleck, the outcome of which shifted the bull's eye from Richmond to Lee's army. Grant said it succinctly in his directive to Meade: "Lee's Army will be your objective point. Wherever Lee goes there you will go also." At first glance, the campaign's execution suggests that, like his predecessors, Grant was driving for Richmond, but the new commander understood that Lee's obligation to defend the Rebel capital would immobilize the southerners and deny them strategic initiative, if not tactical flexibility. This had in fact always been the case, but previous generals had lacked either the strategic vision to make Lee their true objective or the strength of will to seize onto Lee's army and not let go until one side or the other could fight no more. Grant would do just that.[15]

If promotion to the pinnacle of the U.S. military establishment or taking center stage in the high-profile eastern theater had rattled Grant or affected his demeanor, it did not show in his approach to command. There was no arrogance, no bedazzlement with the fawning attentions of a capital city desperate for a general who would deliver victory; instead, there was the same steady, quiet, self-assured commander who had first emerged in Missouri three years and a lifetime ago. As in the West at Fort Donelson, at Vicksburg, and at Chattanooga, Grant believed he would win in the East, no matter how long it took or what unforeseen obstacles might arise. "This confidence," Adam Badeau, one of Grant's aides-de-camp, recalled, "never deserted him." In his last note to the president before launching the campaign, Grant expressed his thanks for the administration's unqualified support and averred, "Should my success be less than I desire, . . . the least I can say is, the fault is not with you." These final words must have brought to Lincoln's mind the tribulations he had suffered with generals all too ready to lay blame on anyone except themselves for their shortcomings and failures. Everything Grant had done since coming east could only have pleased the president, but the coming weeks would tell whether the general from the West was indeed the man capable of winning the war.[16]

As April 1864 passed and the Union armies made final preparations for the impending campaign, Grant acknowledged that the North harbored great expectations of him and that, once news spread of the army's movement south, the pressure to succeed would only intensify. But he trusted in his experience and success, never having been "placed where I lost my presence of mind," except, he awkwardly admitted, "in strange company, particularly of ladies." To his theater commanders, he sent a stern reminder that "hostile armies, and not cities," were their objectives and that "in cases of great emergency . . . urge immediate action, looking to cooperation, without

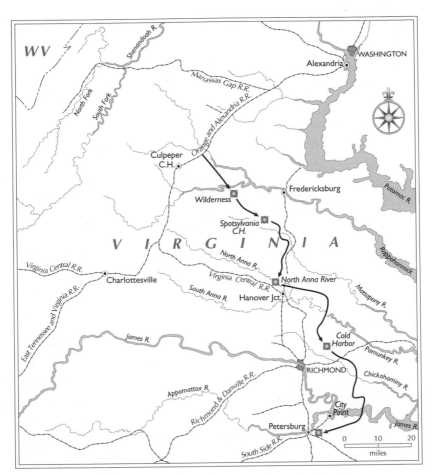

Map 4. The Overland campaign

waiting for specific orders from me." Coordination and commitment would bring victory; "all will strike together."[17]

"The crossing of the Rapidan [River] effected. Forty-eight hours now will demonstrate whether the enemy intends giving battle this side of Richmond." So telegraphed Grant to General Halleck on May 4, 1864. The previous day, the ponderous Army of the Potomac had lurched into motion as soldiers and wagons set off south toward Richmond, and waiting, watching, somewhere in between, was Lee's

Army of Northern Virginia. Two days later, the Yankees were across the river and moving through the haunting forests of the Wilderness, where just a year earlier the same armies had clashed in the Battle of Chancellorsville, Lee's masterpiece of maneuver. Now Grant wanted to move quickly, clear the dense thickets and narrow roads that would negate his advantages in manpower and artillery. Lee too understood the workings of the Wilderness and so immediately set in motion Richard Ewell's and A. P. Hill's two corps with the hopes of opening an attack from the west while Grant was still tangled in the underbrush; James Longstreet's corps followed a day's march behind. Federal cavalry reported that the Confederates were on the move, leading Grant to prompt Meade, "If an opportunity presents itself for pitching into a part of Lee's army, do so without giving time for dispositions." This was exactly the kind of opportunity for which Grant was looking, the chance "to take the initiative whenever the enemy could be drawn from his intrenchments [sic]," and, by moving to attack, Lee was of necessity out of his entrenchments.[18]

The following day, May 5, 1864, the armies were locked in a murderous, chaotic fistfight. Dense vegetation, narrow winding roads, and smoke from muskets and brush fires contributed to hours of confusing and uncoordinated attacks and counterattacks, with neither side able to edge out a decisive advantage. For the most part, Grant allowed Meade a free hand, only occasionally stepping in to take direct control, as when Gen. Gouverneur K. Warren repeatedly delayed advancing his Fifth Corps as ordered. By the end of the day, both armies had been bloodied, but neither Lee nor Grant was willing to back down, Lee anticipating the arrival of Longstreet's lead division by morning, and Grant sensing a weakness in the Rebel line. Ambrose Burnside's Federal Ninth Corps had not engaged, and, believing that they would be sufficient to counter Longstreet's imminent arrival, Grant ordered the attack resumed at 4:30 A.M., just before dawn on May 6. Meade objected, citing the army's disorganization and exhaustion, and requested a delay until 6:00. Grant agreed to a 5:00 A.M. start but no later as he "was afraid if delayed until 6, the enemy would take the initiative which he desires especially to avoid."

As at Fort Donelson and Shiloh, Grant was correct in his assessment that both armies were equally disorganized and that therefore, as at Donelson, "the one who attacks first now will be victorious." Moreover, he either sensed or understood far better than his predecessors the dangers of surrendering the initiative to General Lee.[19]

As morning light began filtering through the oaks and maples of the Wilderness, the battle resumed in earnest. Yankee infantry surged forward, looking to secure a quick finish before Longstreet's corps could throw its full weight into the fight, but Old Pete's men came in at the double-quick, steeling Lee's right flank to keep it from being turned. Bluecoat and butternut then settled into another brawl marked by confusion, chaos, and high casualties. For most of the day, Grant could be found sitting at his headquarters, a stump somewhat to the rear, enveloped in a cloud of cigar smoke while he monitored battle reports and whittled away stick after stick. As noon approached, Confederate artillery thumped close enough to send men scurrying but drew little notice from Grant. A junior officer suggested to the general that it might be prudent to withdraw to a safer distance, to which Grant countered that perhaps "it would be better to order up some artillery and defend the present location." Cannon were soon in place putting down counterbattery fire.[20]

By early evening of the battle's second day, when it seemed that both armies were nearing the limit of their endurance, Richard Ewell's Confederates hit hard John Sedgwick's corps on the Union right flank. Panic swept over a number of the Federals' senior leaders, who were all too familiar with this storyline from their previous encounters with Lee. One frantic brigadier sought to enlighten General Grant, who by all appearances had failed to grasp both the gravity of the situation and the reputation of his Confederate counterpart. The young general blurted out in rapid-fire fashion, "This is a crisis that cannot be looked upon too seriously. I know Lee's methods well by past experience; he will throw his whole army between us and the Rapidan, and cut us off completely." Grant had finally heard enough. "I am heartily tired," he fumed at the officer, "of hearing about what Lee is going to do. Some of you always seem to think he is suddenly going to turn a double somersault, and land in our rear and on both flanks at the same time. Go back to your command, and try to think what we are going to do ourselves, instead of what Lee is going to do." Earlier in the war, at Belmont and Shiloh, Grant's failure to consider what his opponent might have up his sleeve had nearly led to disaster, but by 1864 he had learned from those experiences. According to Sherman, what separated Grant from other commanders at this stage of the war was that, "while they were thinking so much about what the enemy was going to do, Grant was thinking all the time about what he was going to do himself," a quality now made more effective by his consideration of the enemy's intent. Late in the day on May 6, after two days of some of the war's hardest fighting, Grant's assessment proved correct—the Rebels were exhausted, their attack had lost steam, and he was not about to surrender the initiative. He was not going to retreat, and jittery Union brigadiers had best realize this sooner rather than later. Grant did not yet know the Army of the Potomac's generals, and they did not know him, this westerner who had battled only the likes of Pemberton and Bragg, barely competent bumblers compared to the legendary Lee. The Wilderness fight left no doubt that the Army of the Potomac had a new commander, one who saw Lee simply as another opponent who stood between the Union army and final victory.[21]

In Washington, few details had made their way back to the capital while the two armies were engaged. The president, fretful as he awaited word from the front, commented to his secretary John Hay, likely as much to reassure himself as to convince Hay, "The great thing about Grant is his perfect coolness and persistency of purpose. . . . He is not easily excited . . . and he had the grit of a bulldog." A short while later, Lincoln's hopes and expectations for his new commander were confirmed when Henry Wing, a reporter from the *New York Tribune*, appeared at the White House with a personal message from Grant: "If you see the President, tell him from me that whatever happens, there will be no turning back." Lincoln could not have been more relieved, more gratified, or more thankful to get this news from his new commander.[22]

On the morning of May 7, less than twelve hours after the failed Confederate attack on his right flank, Grant issued orders for the army to prepare for a night march. The men in the ranks had heard this song before, and they knew the verses well: march south, get into a brawl with Lee's Rebels, take a beating, and then slink back north to lick their wounds. As the troops fell into line, the column snaked its way eastward, with the bluecoats anticipating the left-hand turn that would take them north to Washington, but as they approached the crossroads the ranks veered, not to the left, but to the right, and at that moment the men knew—there would be no turning back, there would be no retreat. They were pressing on toward Richmond and on in pursuit of Lee. "Our spirits rose," recalled one soldier. "We marched free. The men began to sing." Another soldier observed, "[Grant] looks as if he would stay with 'em till somebody cried enough." The veteran soldier Elisha Hunt Rhodes agreed: "If we were under any other General except Grant I should expect a retreat, but Grant is not that kind of soldier, and we feel that we can trust him." Then, in a scene reminiscent of Napoléon's firelight procession prior to the Battle of Austerlitz, soldiers lit torches to illuminate the way and cheered as Grant rode along the column on his immense horse, Cincinnati. The outburst, his aide Horace Porter believed, was the troops' "emphatic verdict" on their new commander.[23]

Lincoln had brought Grant east and elevated him to high command in anticipation of a new direction for the war, especially a change in the performance and self-confidence of the Army of the Potomac. In the Wilderness, Grant delivered. His old command, the Army of the Tennessee, which had endured Fort Donelson, Shiloh, Vicksburg, and Chattanooga, was accustomed to winning and expected to do so each time battle was imminent. The Army of the Potomac, in sharp contrast, had not the self-confidence that brings consistent victory. This began to change in the Wilderness. In the ranks, men like Elisha Rhodes discovered a renewed commitment to the fight and a leader they could trust. Officers like Horace Porter saw something they had not seen in their previous commanders, a general who "never once doubted his ability to make a forward movement as the result of battle." In the thickets of the Wilderness, the newsman Sylvanus Cadwallader likened his realization of the depth of Grant's will to win as "the grandest sunburst of my life. I had suddenly emerged from the slough of despond, to the solid bed-rock of unwavering faith." As for the Confederates, Grant's performance had confirmed the fears of Lt. Gen. James Longstreet, who had known Grant for decades and warned his colleagues, "We cannot afford to underrate [Grant] and the army he now commands. We must make up our minds to get into line of battle and stay there; for that man will fight us every day and every hour till the end of the war." Writing after the war, Sherman observed that the bloody nose the Federals received in the Wilderness did not diminish Grant's determination: "Undismayed, with a full comprehension of the importance of the work in which he was engaged, . . . he gave his orders calmly, specifically, and absolutely— 'Forward to Spotsylvania.'"[24]

While he did not know the severity, Grant knew that the Confederates had inflicted significant casualties on his army, but he also knew that his men had returned the favor, perhaps more so. Lee showed no signs of retreat or of emerging from his now formidable entrenchments. Grant decided to forgo another frontal assault and instead execute a turning maneuver around Lee's right flank, where he anticipated the threat to the Confederates' supply line would draw Lee out into the open. As he had in the West, Grant demonstrated that his tactics stemmed not from unthinking stubbornness but from analytical determination. At Vicksburg, after two calculated attempts to fight his way into the river stronghold, he chose siege operations to prevent the needless loss of life. Now in the Wilderness, facing a well-entrenched opponent of extraordinary skill, he again opted against direct attack and sought the opportunities of an exposed flank.[25]

On May 8, as the Federal army made its way east, then south, Lee, unsure whether his Yankee opponents were retreating or moving forward, shifted troops southeast to the road junction of Spotsylvania Court House to either block a Federal advance or be in position to strike the enemy's rear. By the next day, Lee's men had thrown up substantial fieldworks and turned back probing attacks on their right and left by Winfield Hancock's and Ambrose Burnside's corps; worse for the Union cause, Gen. John Sedgwick fell mortally wounded during the day's skirmishing. When dawn came on May 10, Grant, looking to overcome the preceding day's setbacks, issued orders for an assault against what he perceived to be the weak center of Lee's line. He followed up with a telegram to Halleck asking for "all the infantry you can rake and scrape," at the same time reiterating that, despite a Rebel force that showed no signs of quitting, the campaign would continue: "The enemy hold our front in very strong force and evince strong determination to interpose between us and Richmond to the last. I shall take no backward steps. . . . We can . . . beat Lee's army." The attack began soon after, but poor coordination among the Yankee corps commanders resulted in piecemeal assaults that allowed the Confederates to meet each hammer blow with equal force. Later that afternoon, after now five days of offensive misfires, effective Rebel counterstrokes, and high casualties, Grant succumbed to a rare expression of frustration and a hint of self-doubt. "I do not know," he told the newsman Charles Coffin, "any way to put down this rebellion and restore the authority of the Government except by fighting, and fighting means that men must be killed. If the people of this country expect that the war can be conducted to a successful issue in any other way than by fighting, they must get somebody other than myself to command the army."[26]

Heavy rains the following day gave both armies a much welcomed respite, and for Grant the dreary weather had a restorative effect as well, evidenced by an early morning telegram to Secretary of War Stanton that was all optimism and fight. Putting a positive spin on his encounters with Lee, he assured Stanton that the previous days of hard fighting had gone in their favor and that, while Union forces had suffered considerable losses, the enemy had surely lost more. Perhaps most important, there would be no change in strategy: "I propose to fight it out on this line if it takes all summer." Orders then went out to Meade to prepare for a resumption of the fight at dawn, with Burnside and Hancock to strike Lee's right and center while Gouverneur K. Warren and Horatio G. Wright looked for an opportunity to hit his left. "Push in if any opportunity presents itself," Grant instructed Meade. To Burnside, the most questionable of his corps commanders, Grant sent word to press the attack "with all possible vigor" and had two of his staff officers deliver the message with orders to remain with Burnside throughout the coming fight; Grant wanted neither confusion nor dilly-dallying generals to undermine the attack at its critical moment.[27]

The Potomac veterans moved out the next morning, May 12, through an opaque gauze of mist and rain before smashing into a bulge in the Confederate line, soon known as the "mule shoe." An initial Yankee breakthrough showed promise of splitting Lee's army down its very center, but quick-acting and hard-driving Confederates plugged the gap, initiating what would become a rain-soaked, daylong stalemate of hand-to-hand fighting in a broth of mud and blood. From his headquarters, Grant repeatedly admonished Burnside to "push the attack as vigorously as possible," and, when Burnside reported that he had lost contact with Hancock's corps to his right, he reiterated, "Push the enemy with all your might; that's the way to connect." On the other end of the line, Warren showed a similar reluctance, and by midmorning Meade had warned Grant of the corps commander's hesitation. "If Warren fails to attack promptly," came Grant's immediate reply, "send [Andrew A.] Humphreys to command his corps and relieve him." As Meade's chief of staff, Humphreys had considerable combat experience and was known for his "distinguished and brilliant profanity," just the man needed to light a fire under the Fifth Corps. For the moment, however, Warren's relief proved unnecessary as both he and Burnside eventually set their men in motion, inspired by Grant's urgings. A rainy twilight brought to a close one of the war's most brutal days, with virtually no change in the armies' dispositions. Lee's southerners, clinging tenaciously to their entrenchments, knew that they had been in a fight, with one Louisiana soldier admitting that now the enemy had a commander "who either does not know when he is whipped, or who cares not if he loses his whole Army, so that he may accomplish an end." A North Carolinian cut right to the point: "Old Grant is certainly a very stubborn fighter."

For their part, Grant's men collected their dead and wounded with the knowledge that the bloodletting was far from over.[28]

More rain on May 13 brought at least a temporary break from the carnage of the previous week and allowed Grant a moment to cable Secretary of War Stanton recommendations to promote Meade and Sherman to the permanent rank of major general in the regular army. Sherman's record spoke for itself, and Grant gave due credit to the Army of the Potomac commander, who had "more than met my most sanguine expectations." Grant may also have hoped that the promotion would steel Meade after the loss of so many men and with the anticipation of casualties still to come. He then turned to the immediate situation at Spotsylvania, where Lee remained firmly lodged in his entrenchments. Grant was fearful that, despite the swamplike roads that led south, Lee might slip away and reach the more formidable fortifications surrounding Richmond, thereby denying the Yankees an opportunity to inflict a fatal blow. In another example of his analytical determination, he rejected the idea of a headlong charge into the teeth of the Confederate defenses at Spotsylvania, even though his men had come within a hair's breadth of cracking Lee's army the previous day. He told Meade that he did not want "a battle brought on with the enemy in their position of yesterday," but instead, as he had done so effectively during the Vicksburg campaign, he would turn again to maneuver and "get by the right flank of the enemy for the next fight."[29]

Writing the same day that he told Meade of his intentions to circle Lee's flank, Grant confessed to his wife, "The world has never seen so bloody or so protracted a battle as the one being fought and I hope never will again. The enemy were really whipped yesterday but their situation is desperate beyond anything heretofore known." The Confederates would at some point reach their breaking point, although when that time would come no one knew. Until then, Grant was going to stay true to the philosophy he first implemented during the Fort Donelson campaign: pressing the fight to its conclusion now will produce fewer casualties than a protracted war of battle and retreat.[30]

The middle days of May saw the same dreary, rain-soaked weather that had plagued the two armies for some time, but they continued to carry on intermittent skirmishing as the Rebels waited for Grant's next move. Grant, fearful that the stalled campaign would set Lincoln and Stanton to thinking he was losing his resolve, telegraphed his assurances that "the army is in the best of spirits and feel greatest confidence in ultimate success" and that only the foul weather had slowed the push against Lee, not "weakness or exhaustion on our part." While Grant had told Meade a few days earlier of his intentions to swing around Lee's right flank, he did not issue the orders until May 18. By then, he had received word from Halleck that Siegel's campaign in the Shenandoah Valley and Butler's push along the James River had failed miserably. Gray-clad columns would soon be on the march to reinforce Lee instead of moving to those other theaters. This, Grant recalled, was "no time for repining," so orders went out to begin wheeling around the Union left flank, avoiding a general engagement unless "the enemy will come out of their works to fight." With the Army of the Potomac on the move, Lee's men would have to do likewise.[31]

Winfield Scott Hancock's Second Corps headed the Federal army as it made its way south. Hancock's men slipped past Lee's flank on the way to the North Anna River, which they reached the evening of May 23. There they found that once again Lee's army was the quicker, having arrived first, crossed the river, and established a firm line of defense; nevertheless, both Hancock's and Warren's corps pressed on to the south riverbank, meeting at best moderate resistance. The following morning revealed to Grant, if he had not come to appreciate it before, the extraordinary quality of his opponent. Lee had deployed his men in an inverted *V*, with the point resting near the river and the sides running roughly southwest and southeast, a position that split the Yankees in half as soon as they crossed the river and prevented each Federal force from supporting the other. Grant immediately saw the risk of going forward, so he ordered Meade to break contact and get the army moving again around Lee's right flank. He explained to Halleck, "To make a direct attack from either wing would cause a slaughter of our men that even success would not justify." Union veterans who had survived the recent days of incessant fighting knew all too well the dangers of an entrenched Confederate and so recognized that Grant's decision to sidestep a battle had "saved them on the North Anna from slaughter." They also knew that their tactical withdrawal was not a strategic retreat, that they would continue the push south. "General," one Yankee soldier told Grant as he rode past the column on May 27, "we'll lick 'em sure pop next time." As the War Department official Charles Dana observed, the Army of the Potomac "has learned to believe that it is sure of victory. Even our officers have ceased to regard Lee as an invincible military genius," a newfound confidence that the army's commander recognized: "Our men feel that they have gained the morale over the enemy and attack with confidence." Back in Washington, the president's confidence in his general-in-chief remained unshaken: "It is the dogged pertinacity of Grant that wins."[32]

Just a few days later, the Union army had moved closer still to Richmond, crossing the Pamunkey River near Hanovertown on May 29, and slipping past Lee's blocking move at Totopotomy Creek on the thirtieth. Belying what was to come, Charles Dana reported to Secretary of War Stanton, "General Grant means to fight here if there is a fair chance, but he will not run his head against heavy works." On May 30, Phil Sheridan's cavalry rode into the crossroads town of Cold Harbor, hardly a mile from the 1862 Gaines' Mill battlefield, and fought a delaying action long enough for Wright's Sixth Corps bluecoats to add their weight to the fight and secure the position. Arriving in the area that afternoon, Grant sensed an opportunity. Lee had failed to launch his customary counterattacks at the North Anna River, and his movements had been uncharacteristically slow from the river to Cold Harbor, suggesting that four weeks of relentless battle and mounting casualties had perhaps stretched the Rebels to their breaking point. Orders went out to corps commanders to prepare for a dawn assault that just might catch Lee before he could entrench or fall back to Richmond's fortifications. The attack, however, was not to be. By the morning of June 2, a significant portion of the army was still on the march or just arriving at Cold Harbor, slowed by darkness, narrow and confusing roads, excessive heat and dust, and their own accumulated fatigues from weeks of fighting. Grant delayed the attack until that afternoon but soon made the decision that an additional few hours would be insufficient to overcome communication problems among the corps commanders. He reset the assault to step off the following morning, Friday, June 3.[33]

These all too reasonable postponements added up to a cost the Yankees were ill prepared to pay. At 4:30 A.M., the three corps of Hancock, Wright, and W. F. "Baldy" Smith surged forward, sixty thousand strong, into a whirlwind of minie balls and canister spewing from Confederates who were all but invisible behind earthworks thrown up during the previous day's delays. Responding to initial reports that were encouraging but inconclusive, Grant counseled Meade, "The moment it becomes certain that an assault cannot succeed, suspend the offensive; but when one does succeed, push it vigorously and if necessary pile in troops at the successful point." As more definitive reports came in, it became apparent that there would be no piling in of troops as the Confederates repulsed the Federal attack with a ferocity that surpassed even the bloodiest days in the Wilderness and at the Mule Shoe. Seven thousand casualties accumulated in the attack's first ten minutes. By noon, Grant had heard enough from his corps commanders to direct Meade to call off any further attacks. The men were to dig in and hold whatever gains they had made, but officers were admonished to remain alert for any opportunity to strike should the enemy leave their entrenchments.[34]

That evening Grant and the Union high command learned the magnitude of their losses, harrowing additions to the previous month's body count. For his part, Grant recognized that he had made a grievous mistake, telling his staff, "I regret this assault more than any one I have ever ordered. I regarded it as a stern necessity, and believed that it would bring compensating results; but, as it has proved, no advantages have been gained sufficient to justify the heavy losses suffered." As at Vicksburg, Grant believed that, if successful, an immediate assault would have preserved "life, health, and comfort."

Nevertheless, this time his assessment was incorrect, and the decision to assault the fortifications at Cold Harbor was more stubborn than steadfast. After the setbacks and delays of June 2 forced a postponement of the operation, further reconnaissance and reflection might have suggested that the better, although more immediately frustrating path, was to again look to Lee's flanks. Such maneuvering may have maintained the momentum of the advance, without the unwarranted sacrifice of men who in their own right had demonstrated great determination.[35]

Given Cold Harbor's disastrous consequences and Grant's realization that the sacrifices of so many had gained so little, one might well have expected an operational pause to allow the army and its commander to recover and regroup. It should not surprise that Grant never seriously contemplated such a course. Adam Badeau, a colonel on Grant's staff during the campaign, recalled, "Nothing deterred him [or] depressed or discouraged, so far as those nearest him could discover, this imperturbable man. . . . [H]is confidence never wavered. . . . [H]e was yet advancing, not only . . . towards Richmond, but towards the goal he had proposed to himself, the destruction of Lee and the rebellion." Equally important, the Army of the Potomac had internalized their commander's commitment to success, showing the same resolve to see the matter through. A short five days after the cruel harvest of Cold Harbor, a New York soldier wrote, "We have the gray backs in a pretty close corner at present and intend to keep them so. There is no fall back with U. S. Grant." And, because of Grant, there was little fallback in the ranks. Even the dour Meade had taken on some of Grant's steely resolve, writing, "There is a determination on all sides to fight it out, and have an end put to the war."[36]

Writing after the war, Sylvanus Cadwallader recalled the Overland campaign as a time when "like the classic heroes of old Grant had been saying . . . to Lee, . . . 'If you are the general you claim to be, come out and fight me'; and Lee had replied, in like manner: 'If you are the general you are represented to be, compel me to come out and fight you.'" Throughout the month of May 1864, Grant had been unable to draw Lee from his entrenchments into a fight in the open, despite having led the Army of the Potomac on a campaign of maneuver and adaptation that rivaled Vicksburg. The Overland campaign was the most difficult challenge Grant faced during the war, the fight for which his earlier military career had prepared him. The mentoring of men like Charles F. Smith, the self-confidence gained in Missouri, the lessons of command and control from Belmont and Fort Donelson, the decision to fight it out at Shiloh, and the adaptive determination of Vicksburg and Chattanooga had all worked to prepare Grant for this campaign. Robert E. Lee, no Bragg or Pemberton, was an exceptionally worthy opponent who parried his counterpart's every thrust, but Grant was playing the tune to which Lee had to dance. He had set the agenda in early May when the Yankees crossed the Rapidan River, and through constant maneuvering he maintained the initiative, forcing Lee to gradually but surely expend the lifeblood of his army and the southern cause.[37]

When the campaign ended in early June, the war's outcome was still in doubt. Lee remained dangerous, capable of striking a serious blow if Grant faltered, but the Confederate general was committed to the politically necessary but militarily foolish course of defending a city his opponent did not want or need. Richmond was of no consequence to Grant. The Army of Northern Virginia was his objective, and, as the previous month had shown, he would pursue that goal with relentless determination. There was no fallback in U. S. Grant.

7

Richmond, Petersburg, and Peace

> Give him no peace whilst the war lasts.
> —Ulysses S. Grant

The dead of Cold Harbor were still being committed to the earth and God's care when General Grant sent word to Washington that although the nation rightly mourned the fallen he remained fully committed to the unfinished task, to "beat and drive the enemy" into submission. His confidence in his men was unshaken. If only the Rebels would come out of their entrenchments for a stand-up fight, the war would soon be over. Unfortunately for the bluecoats, Robert E. Lee was not about to be caught in the open, a fact that he had demonstrated repeatedly over the last four weeks, and now the Confederates were secure in their fortifications around Richmond, hoping the Yankees would repeat their Cold Harbor performance.

For his part, Grant was not going to undertake another head-long charge into a blaze of musket and artillery fire. As at Vicksburg, where he could have fought a war of attrition by repeated frontal assaults, he could have done so at Richmond and, given the available resources of both armies, he might well have won, albeit at an unthinkable cost. But, at Vicksburg and again at Chattanooga, he had learned the value of logistics and controlling the railroads. He had also learned that once he had secured his own supply line and blocked that of the enemy he could win by siege if necessary. In the recent Overland campaign, Grant had looked for every opportunity to attack Lee's army outside its fortifications, but Lee never gave him that opportunity. Thus, after Cold Harbor, with Lee and his men peering out over parapets studded with abatis and chevaux-de-frise, Grant took inspiration from his Vicksburg success. Looking to hold a line northeast of Richmond, he sidled his army south to the James River and across toward Petersburg, searching out the railroads that fed Richmond and Confederate hopes. Once the Federals had severed those lines, the Rebels would have to starve or flee. If as Grant believed Lee would fight until he could fight no more, this path would be the most efficient way in terms of lives, if not in terms of days, to bring the war to its final conclusion.[1]

In early June, however, Lee's army in flight remained the stuff of late-night musings, but Grant now had a plan to turn those musings into reality, and on June 12 the Army of the Potomac broke camp to continue its southward procession. Two days later, the army began crossing the James River. Grant conferred with Ben Butler in Bermuda Hundred on the possibility of a few thousand or so of Butler's Ninth Corps men joining with Baldy Smith's corps for an immediate attack against Petersburg. Grant believed that he had stolen a march on Lee, and he wanted to strike before the Rebels could shuttle troops from Richmond south to Petersburg. One of Butler's soldiers caught sight of Grant while he was in camp and observed, "I associated with his appearance the idea . . . of a huge ponderous iron roller (on a very slightly inclined plane) which though hard to start yet when once fairly underway by its momentum carried every thing before it and is almost impossible to stop." The army commander certainly had no intentions of stopping, thus his orders for an assault the following morning with Smith's men at the point and Hancock's Second Corps coming up in support. If all went as planned, at dawn on June 15 thirty-five thousand Federals would roll over P. G. T. Beauregard's thin screen of nine thousand Confederates to seize Petersburg and its vital rail hub. On the afternoon of June 14, Grant cabled his plans to Washington; Lincoln's reply came the following morning. He offered his general the best reassurances he could: "Have just received your dispatch of 1 P.M. yesterday. I begin to see it. You will succeed. God bless you all."[2]

For three days, the Army of the Potomac had functioned like the experienced veterans that they were, withdrawing from the enemy's front at Cold Harbor, and transiting to the James with efficiency and drive. Still, old habits die hard, and at a moment of grand opportunity the army, or more appropriately its commanders, stumbled. On June 15, as the Eighteenth Corps prepared to give battle, Baldy Smith rode forward to get a feel for the terrain and Confederate defenses. Understandably gun shy after the disaster at Cold Harbor, he wanted no surprises. What he saw was less than encouraging. Formidable entrenchments and artillery positions covered every inch of a wide killing field, but Smith nevertheless decided that there was an opportunity here if the attack moved quickly, before Lee's reinforcements could reach the area. Yet a quick assault was not to be when miscommunication and misunderstandings delayed the initial bombardment until seven o'clock that evening. The Federals then surged forward. They charged across the open ground and soon, to their surprise and relief, found themselves inside the Confederates' lines. With a suddenness expected by no one, the previous occupants were now either prisoners or scampering back toward Petersburg. Everything seemed to be falling into place for the Yankees—the thinly held southern defenses had been cracked, Lee's men were still miles away north of town, and Hancock's corps was finally up, waiting only for the order to move. Petersburg and the rail hub on which Richmond relied were there for the taking; but then Smith faltered. Unprepared, or more precisely unwilling, to undertake night operations, and believing that Lee's reinforcements must surely be in Petersburg by now, the Eighteenth Corps's commander called off the attack. Hancock had just arrived on the field with his corps and was therefore in no position to challenge Smith's assessment, so he acquiesced to the decision.[3]

Grant had spent the day at his new headquarters at City Point, on the James River, monitoring reports from the front, and keeping an eye on Butler's position at Bermuda Hundred in case Lee attacked there. Smith's attack had come so late on the fifteenth that Grant did not make it out to the battlefield until early the next morning, where, after an evaluation of the terrain and the previous day's progress, he determined that, as with the situation at Vicksburg a year earlier, a second attack was warranted. Crossing paths with Meade between the front and City Point, he issued orders for a full offensive that evening at 6:00, with Gouverneur Warren's corps joining those of Smith and Hancock. A quick victory, however, was not to be. The evening attacks gained little of substance as southern forces had finally arrived in significant numbers and the men in blue were laboring under an accumulated six weeks of relentless combat. A faint optimism still flickered in Grant on June 17 and 18, but more uncoordinated and halfhearted attacks, poor performances from corps commanders, and increasingly formidable Confederate fortifications snuffed out any hope of taking Petersburg but by siege. Grant acknowledged as much to Meade, pronouncing, "I am perfectly satisfied that all has been done that could be done."[4]

Over the previous five weeks, Grant had incurred in excess of eleven thousand casualties, more than his army had endured in the entire Vicksburg campaign, and still he had not captured Richmond or even Petersburg, let alone knocked Lee's army out of the war. From early May through mid-June, he had maintained the army's strategic momentum, but operational momentum and tactical success often depend on the skill and tenacity of subordinate generals, especially the corps commanders, and during this phase of the campaign those commanders came up short. Grant must also shoulder some of the responsibility for having failed to instill in his officers his own determination to exploit every mistake or opportunity the enemy offered. In his memoir, he reflected on the squandered opportunities of those mid-June days, writing, "I believed then, and still believe, that Petersburg could have been easily captured at that time." Nevertheless, despite a possible missed opportunity, the Federals had denied Lee the initiative, robbed him of the freedom to maneuver, and maintained relentless pressure on a brittle Confederate supply system.[5]

If Grant suffered from any disappointment at being unable to establish his headquarters in downtown Petersburg, he did not reveal it to his men, who for their part sustained a confident faith in their commander. Capt. Charles F. Adams reassured his father, "Grant will take Richmond, if only he is left alone, of that I feel more and more sure. His tenacity and strength, combined with his skill, must, on every general principle, prove too much for them in the end." A Union navy man wryly observed, "When Grant gets possession of a place, he holds on to it as if he had inherited it." Sherman recalled, "I knew Grant would make the fur fly when he started down through Virginia. . . . He has all the tenacity of a Scotch terrier. . . . When Grant cried 'Forward!' after the battle of the Wilderness, I said: 'This is the grandest act of his life; now I feel that the rebellion will be crushed.'" Most important, President Lincoln also maintained his unwavering faith in Grant as a leader and a strategist, and reaffirmed his own commitment to following the course Grant had laid out. Addressing a crowd at the Philadelphia Sanitary Commission fair on June 16, while the assaults on Petersburg were under way, Lincoln told the audience, "General Grant is reported to have said, 'I am going through on this line if it takes all summer.' I say we are going through on this line if it takes three more years." Back in the field, the president's recommitment to the cause could not have been better timed to buck up Grant, for on June 18 he had come to accept that the opportunity for a quick capture of Petersburg had passed. Unless he was prepared to sacrifice the Army of the Potomac in suicidal frontal assaults, he would again have to begin the tedious work of siege operations. Fortunately for the Union cause, Lincoln and Grant remained of like minds. The general told the president, "You will never hear of me farther from Richmond than now, till I have taken it. I am just as sure of going into Richmond as I am of any future event. It may take a long summer day, as they say in the rebel papers, but I will do it." On June 20, Lincoln visited Grant at his City Point headquarters, where their relationship matured as they conferred on coming operations. Secretary of the Navy Gideon Wells recalled that, on the president's return to Washington, his physical appearance had noticeably improved and that he seemed "strengthened . . . mentally." By pressing the enemy, Grant had finally eased the anxiety that had plagued Lincoln in his search for a commander. The president and his general had again

committed themselves to each other and a shared strategy that would
in the end determine the outcome of the war.[6]

As the Petersburg siege devolved into a war of trenches, Grant
also had the responsibility as general-in-chief of keeping his hand on
operations elsewhere. "It kept me pretty active in looking after all
these points," Grant recalled of the summer of 1864. Being engaged
in a chess game with Lee was more than sufficient work for any man,
and one could understand a commanding general looking to pass off
the management of other campaigns and their balky generals to Chief
of Staff Halleck, but Grant never contemplated such an abdication
of his responsibilities. His aide Horace Porter likened Grant's task
of overseeing the Union's various armies to steering a team of four
horses, "a dashing four-in-hand," with the driver pulling, cajoling,
and at times whipping to keep them working in harmony.[7]

Soon after the armies began settling into siege operations, Confederate general Jubal Early put a scare into Washington. He struck
out north across the Potomac with around fourteen thousand soldiers and then turned east toward the capital, where Union defenses
had been stripped to fill the ranks for the previous two months' campaign. On July 9, Lew Wallace, who had fought with Grant at Shiloh
two years earlier, attempted to stop the charging Early at Monocacy,
Maryland, but did little more than slow the Rebel advance. Washington was now in a panic, and every administration official, including
the president, looked to Grant for relief. He began shuttling reinforcements north but declined to comply with Lincoln's request to
oversee the defense of the city himself. Grant recognized Early's raid
for what it was, more show than substance, and his primary objective still lay in his front at Petersburg; in fact, he believed that taking
Early's bait was "probably just what Lee wants me to do." On July
11, Old Jube's luck ran out. He collided with entrenchments manned
by veterans of the Sixth Corps, whose commander, Horatio Wright,
saw an opportunity to amputate a powerful limb of Lee's army. Grant
sent orders to "push the enemy in Maryland with all vigor, to make
a bold campaign against him, and destroy him if possible." Although
Early evaded his pursuers and scampered back south across the Po-

tomac, Grant had correctly assessed the gravity of the threat and responded appropriately, all while keeping his eye on the objective of Lee and the main Rebel army.[8]

Yet the troublesome Early, whom Lee referred to as "my bad old man," was not so easily dissuaded, and, as soon as the pursuing Federals turned back north, he again waded the Potomac into the Shenandoah Valley. Since Stonewall Jackson's Valley campaign in the early summer of 1862, the Confederates had repeatedly sustained their armies by drawing on the generous farmlands that dotted the Shenandoah's countryside. Now two summers later, the Rebels were still in the valley, and Grant had had enough. To clear the valley once and for all, he turned to an officer who had shown a resolve equal to his own. On August 1, 1864, from his headquarters at City Point, Grant telegraphed Halleck, "[I want Phil] Sheridan put in command of all the troops in the [Shenandoah Valley] with instructions to put himself south of the enemy and follow him to the death. Wherever the enemy goes let our troops go also." Despite the clarity of these orders, Grant received a warning from the president that, if Grant himself did not ensure the transmission of his orders to Sheridan, they would likely become entangled in the bureaucratic web woven by Halleck and Secretary of War Stanton. "I repeat to you," Lincoln cabled on August 3, "it will neither be done nor attempted unless you watch it every day, and hour, and force it." Grant appreciated the veracity of Lincoln's warning and was soon on his way north, not to Washington, but to meet Sheridan in person to make explicit his intentions for the campaign. Meeting in Monocacy, Maryland, Grant told Sheridan that he wanted the valley cleared, not just of Confederates, but of anything and everything that might draw them back. This reiterated his message of two weeks earlier: "The enemy . . . should have upon his heels, veterans, Militiamen, men on horseback and everything that can be got to follow, to eat out Virginia clear and clean . . . so that crows flying over [the valley] . . . will have to carry their provender with them." Then a final word: "What we want is prompt and active movements after the enemy." Somewhat surprisingly, despite these explicit instructions Sheridan failed to move, forcing Grant to repeat his orders to make the Shenandoah Valley a "barren waste." Once finally under way, Little Phil hit hard, striking a series of blows against Early's corps at Opequon Creek, Fisher's Hill, and, finally, Cedar Creek on October 19, 1864. With a little prodding from Grant, Sheridan had at last swept the valley of Lee's tough and tenacious "bad old man."[9]

Earlier in August, while he was defining the parameters of the Valley campaign for Sheridan, Grant received a disturbing telegram from Halleck of trouble brewing in New York, Pennsylvania, and other states over the unpopular conscription law. Opposition was intensifying, and Halleck feared that "a forcible resistance" would "require the withdrawal of a very considerable number of troops from the field. . . . Are not the appearances such that we ought to take in sail and prepare the ship for a storm?" Grant would have none of it. "If we are to draw troops from the field," he notified Halleck on August 15, "to keep the loyal states in the harness it will prove difficult to suppress the rebellion in the disloyal states." Moreover, shifting troops away from Richmond would give Lee the opportunity to send reinforcements to Atlanta, where Sherman was already hard-pressed. In this instance, northern governors would have to rely on their militia to maintain civil order as he was not about to have troops and attention diverted from the war's center of gravity—Lee's army at Richmond. The final arbiter was of course the president, who had to consider not only the war at the front and potential unrest in the rear but also the looming fall elections, including his own campaign for a second term. Grant received Lincoln's response on August 17, 1864, and the president's position was unequivocal: "I have seen your dispatch expressing your unwillingness to break your hold where you are. Neither am I willing. Hold on with a bull-dog gripe [*sic*], and chew and choke, as much as possible." The president and his general remained in agreement that Lee's army was the paramount objective and that reacting to every potential crisis would jeopardize the war effort. The president was standing firm, but Grant worried over public impatience to see the war end, telling Elihu Washburne that victory was likely only "if we will but be true to ourselves."[10]

Yet another possible crisis that confronted Grant in the fall of 1864 arose in Central Tennessee, whose people and geography he had come to know well during the 1862 spring campaign of Forts Henry and Donelson and the capture of Nashville. Now, more than two years later, the state capital was once again threatened, this time by John Bell Hood and his Confederate Army of Tennessee, which was making a dash north. They looked to defeat Union forces led by George H. Thomas, and then, with an optimism that belied reality, Hood planned to trek east to reinforce Lee's beleaguered army at Richmond. Despite a severe thrashing at the Battle of Franklin on November 30, 1864, which saw the death of six Confederate generals, Hood pressed on to Thomas's defensive works shielding Nashville. His advance into Tennessee had created something of a panic in Washington, and the pressure on Grant to act increased. He too was becoming increasingly concerned with this southern offensive and prodded Thomas to strike Hood to "annihilate him in the open field" before the Confederates besieged the city. Thomas, though a master of defense, took to the offensive with slow deliberation, and, now facing a wounded but still dangerous foe, he was not going to be pressured into a premature attack. On December 2, Secretary of War Stanton relayed to Grant the president's assessment that the situation seemed like "the McClellan and Rosecranz [*sic*] strategy of do nothing and let the rebels raid the country. The President wishes you to consider the matter." The comparison to McClellan and Rosecrans surely stung Grant, and, recalling Thomas's hesitations at Chattanooga, he was himself losing patience with the recalcitrant army commander.[11]

With increasing agitation, Grant fired off a series of telegrams pushing Thomas to attack:

December 2: "You will now suffer incalculable injury upon your Rail Roads if Hood is not speedily disposed of, put forth therefore every possible exertion to attain this end. . . . [G]ive him no peace."

December 5: "Hood should be attacked where he is. Time strengthens him in all possibility as much as it does you."

December 6: "Attack Hood at once and wait no longer."

December 8: "Why not attack at once? . . . Now is one of the farest [sic] opportunities ever presented of destroying one of the three Armies of the enemy. If destroyed he never can replace it."

At one point, Grant cabled Halleck that it was time to consider a change in command and recommended, "If Thomas has not struck yet he ought to be ordered to hand over his command to [Maj. Gen. John] Schofield. There is no better man to repel an attack than Thomas —but I fear he is too cautious to ever take the initiative." This was a rare moment when Grant appeared unwilling to make a difficult call, something Halleck immediately recognized, responding, "If you wish Genl Thomas relieved from command, give the order. No one here will, I think, interfere. The responsibility, however, will be yours." With Halleck unwilling to do his dirty work, Grant backed down, but word now reached his headquarters that bad weather in Tennessee might cause even further delays. "If you delay attack longer," he wired Thomas, "the mortifying spectacle will be witnessed of a Rebel Army moving for the Ohio River. . . . Delay no longer for weather or reinforcements." When Thomas argued that ice precluded the army's movement, Grant had heard enough. On December 13, he ordered Gen. John Logan, who had served as a division commander during the Vicksburg campaign, to Nashville with instructions to take command of Federal forces if Thomas had not moved; a short time later, Grant decided that the matter had to be dealt with personally and so set off for Nashville. During a stopover in Washington on December 15, good news finally arrived from Thomas: the weather had cleared, and his men had struck Hood's southerners a terrific blow, sending them reeling back south. Grant was delighted but, fearing the Rebels might escape, ordered Thomas, "Push the enemy now and give him no rest until he is entirely destroyed. . . . Do not stop for trains or supplies but take them from the country as the enemy has done. Much is now expected." Thomas was unable to inflict the coup de grâce that Grant wanted, but the end result proved sufficient as Hood's decimated army retreated into Mississippi and irrelevance for the remainder of the war.[12]

Horace Porter recorded that the first two weeks of December 1864 were "the most anxious period of Grant's entire military career" and that "he suffered mental torture." Thomas's reticence had rubbed against Grant's nature and war-fighting philosophy. His frustrations were undoubtedly exacerbated by political pressure from Washington and the rocky relationship that had troubled the two commanders since their run-in at Chattanooga. Moreover, keeping tabs on Thomas and repeatedly spurring him on was a distraction from the war's two primary operations: the Army of the Potomac's ongoing siege at Richmond and Petersburg and Sherman's campaign in Georgia.[13]

Looking back after the war, Sherman recounted Grant's strategy for 1864 simply enough: "He was to go for Lee and I was to go for Joe Johnston. That was the plan." In early May, as Grant began going after Lee, crossing the Rapidan River and driving toward their meeting in the Wilderness, Sherman struck south from Chattanooga with Atlanta and its defenders, Joseph E. Johnston and the Army of Tennessee, in his crosshairs. From the Battle of Rocky Face Ridge to the Federal charge at Kennesaw Mountain in late June, the Yankees pushed forward for seven weeks, looking for the fatal error in generalship that would doom the Rebels. Joe Johnston, however, was a well-worn commander who excelled at fighting withdrawals and not making mistakes. But retreat is still retreat, and Jefferson Davis saw little to be gained from Johnston's tactics, no matter how masterful a withdrawal he was able to orchestrate. Looking for a replacement, Davis settled on Gen. John Bell Hood, who had a reputation for audacity and aggressiveness, exactly what the Confederate president believed necessary for a spirited defense of Atlanta. Hood's penchant for bold action and leading from the front had cost him the use of his right arm at Gettysburg and the complete loss of his right leg from a near mortal wound at Chickamauga. None of these sacrifices, however, had cooled his fire for battle, and he did not disappoint; within two days of taking command on July 17, 1864, Hood vigorously and repeatedly struck back at the Federals but in doing so did more damage to his own army than to Sherman's. For his part, Sherman had no plans of altering his course because of Hood and reassured Grant on August 19, "I will never take a step backward and have no fears of Hood. I can whip him outside of his trenches and think in time I can compel him to come out." Sherman's commitment to no retrograde movement surely drew a nod of approval from Grant.[14]

By late August, while Grant was dealing with a possible epidemic of draft riots in the north, Sherman had Hood and Atlanta nearly encircled. Faced with either surrendering the city or sacrificing his army, Hood evacuated Atlanta on September 2, giving Sherman the city, but denying him his main objective of capturing or destroying the army. While Sherman's victory was not complete, it did ensure Lincoln's reelection in November and confirmed Grant's faith in Sherman as a capable army commander. "Our movements were cooperative," Grant said of his best general, "but after starting each have done all that we felt ourselves able to do." Sherman's success also reaffirmed Lincoln's faith in Grant. From the early days of the war, Grant had understood the intimate relationship between war and politics, demonstrated by his toleration of the president's political generals, most notoriously John McClernand, and his recognition that the war's continuation hung on the November elections. The South's only hope, Grant believed, was "in a divided North." They looked "for a counter revolution. They hope for the election of the peace candidate," none other than his predecessor, Gen. George B. McClellan. Now the general-in-chief's patience and political acumen had paid off, along with Sherman's Georgia expedition, by sustaining sufficient Democratic support for Lincoln to win a second term.[15]

Nevertheless, there was more to be done. A short week after the fall of Atlanta, Grant was encouraging Sherman to make immediate preparations for another campaign. "We want to keep the enemy continually pressed to the end of the war," he wrote on September 10. "If we give him no peace whilst the war lasts the end cannot be distant." While Grant's expectations for a quick conclusion were overly optimistic, peace would certainly not come more quickly with hesitation or delay. Within a few days, Sherman proposed a new campaign that would take his army through the Georgia countryside from Atlanta to the coast, "breaking roads and doing irreparable damage" to the Confederates' warmaking resources and their will to carry on the fight. Grant, who identified the enemy's armies as the appropriate center of gravity, was at first skeptical, questioning Sherman if he should not first chase down Hood's elusive army and "entirely settle him before starting on your proposed campaign. . . . If you can see the chance for destroying Hood's Army, attend to that first and make your other move secondary." Sherman countered that that was just what Hood wanted, to lead Sherman's men on a goose chase across the South, and he opposed taking the bait. A more effective alternative, Sherman argued, would be to leave Gen. George Thomas with "a force strong enough to prevent [Hood from] reaching any country in which we have an interest" while the bulk of the army moved east toward Savannah or Charleston on the coast, where it could join with U.S. naval forces. Sherman's reasoning was sound and persuaded Grant. On November 2, he cabled Sherman, "I do not really see that you can withdraw from where you are to follow Hood, without giving up all we have gained in territory. I say, then, go on as you propose." Had he known the headaches that Thomas would create in his jousting with Hood outside Nashville in early December, Grant might have had second thoughts about approving Sherman's plans, but at this point in the war he had come to trust Sherman's judgment. Having fully warmed to the campaign, Grant told a *New York Times* reporter, "The Confederacy is a mere shell. I know it. I am sure of it. It is a hollow shell, and Sherman will prove it to you." On November 15, Sherman and his army headed off into the Georgia countryside. As the days passed and Grant and Lincoln awaited news of the campaign, the president commented to John Sherman, a U.S. senator and the general's brother, "I know what hole he went in at, but I can't tell you what hole he will come out of." On December 10, after a nerve-wracking three weeks for Grant and the president, Sherman finally did emerge at Savannah and moved into the city eleven days later. Sherman's strategic thinking, coupled with Grant's trust and approval, had eliminated meaningful Confederate resistance in Georgia, allowing Sherman to turn northward toward the Carolinas and Virginia, where Grant continued siege operations outside Richmond and Petersburg.[16]

While Grant was directing these various Union campaigns, he also continued to manage his own piece of the war around the Confederate capital, where General Lee had kept him at bay. Always preferring to initiate rather than react to events, Grant poked and prodded Lee's defenses, searching for weaknesses in the line, feeling for a vulnerable flank that might be turned, or scouting to cut yet another rail line. Every action was designed to tighten the vise on the Rebels or break their hold on the cities. On July 27, 1864, for example, he sent Hancock's Second Corps and a good portion of Sheridan's cavalry north of Richmond, their objective being the Virginia Central Railroad, stressing that "if they see the enemy giving away on their front . . . they should take advantage of such knowledge and act promptly without waiting for orders from army commanders." Lee adroitly countered the operation by shifting troops from the Petersburg trenches, but in this setback Grant saw another door open. He telegraphed Halleck, "We have failed in what I had hoped to accomplish. . . . [Nevertheless,] I am yet in hopes of turning this diversion to account so as to yeald [sic] greater results than if the first object had been accomplished."[17]

Lee's shuffling of troops had weakened the defenses south of Petersburg, in the same area where the Yankees were planning something of a surprise. An underground shaft, the work of Pennsylvania soldiers who had been miners prior to the war, angled from the Federal line to below the Rebel entrenchments. The sudden thinning of the southern defenses provided the opportune time to pack the shaft with explosives and blow the remaining Confederates out of the way. At Vicksburg, Grant's men had conducted a similar experiment, with less than notable results; perhaps here the outcome would be more decisive. Just before dawn on July 30, the earth trembled as the charge tore open a crater 150 feet wide and 30 feet deep. Federal soldiers moved into the fog of dust and smoke, ready to take advantage of the surprise and confusion created by the blast. Instead, they paid the price for poor leadership and planning as the operation went badly awry. Rather than moving around the perimeter of the crater to turn the ends of the now exposed Confederate line, the attackers descended into the pit, where they found getting out was far more difficult than getting in. Confederate gunners lobbed in artillery shells, which did their work with grand efficiency. By late morning, Union officers had recalled the survivors, ending what Grant described as "the saddest affair I have witnessed in the war." There was plenty of blame to go around for the disaster, most notably for the lead division's commander, who spent the morning drunk in the rear while his men struggled in the pit. Testifying later before the congressional Joint Committee on the Conduct of the War, Grant declined to pass off responsibility wholly to junior officers and accepted part of the blame himself for failing, along with other senior commanders, to provide more direct oversight for such an important operation. "I think the cause of the disaster," he acknowledged, "was simply the leaving the passage of orders from one to another down to an inefficient man. I blame his seniors also for not seeing that he did his duty, all the way up to myself." The cost of this collective failure in leadership was nearly four thousand Union casualties and the squandering of an opportunity to force Lee to evacuate the Petersburg defenses, a move that he would now be spared from making for another nine months. Lamenting the loss, Grant confessed to Halleck, "Such an opportunity for carrying fortifications I have never seen and do not expect again to have."[18]

Mistakes had been made, but one could not dwell on such failures when the wider war remained to be fought. Sheridan's campaign in the Shenandoah Valley was just getting under way, Sherman was backing Joe Johnston up to Atlanta, and the distant rumblings of the draft protests in New York and Pennsylvania threatened to derail public support and the Richmond front. Although these issues continued to claim their share of his time and energy, as summer turned to fall Grant did not lose sight of his immediate objective of increasing the pressure on Lee's besieged army. In late October 1864, he directed Meade to organize an assault on the Southside Railroad, one of the few remaining feeder lines still open into Petersburg. If the operation was successful, another Confederate artery would be cut, and Lee would again have to draw troops to his right, pulling even harder on a line that was already threatening to snap at any number of points. Winfield Scott Hancock's Second Corps once more was at the point of attack when on October 27 they ran into "obstacles of every conceivable description," both man-made and natural, including thick underbrush, high water, and abatis. Grant had moved forward to observe the operation, in fact coming under fire when an artillery shell exploded just a few feet in front of his horse. From that vantage point, he soon realized the futility of shoving more men into firmly held Confederate fortifications and ordered the withdrawal of Hancock's corps. The Southside Railroad remained open; the siege plodded on.[19]

For a man like Grant, whose philosophy of finding the enemy, striking the enemy, and maintaining the momentum did not lend itself to static warfare, conducting a siege that had lingered for months was a source of mounting frustration. Adding to his irritation were a number of well-meaning but misguided citizens who had their own ideas of how to break the stalemate, designs that they readily shared with the general-in-chief. One industrious engineer submitted architectural drawings detailing the construction of a masonry wall encircling Richmond, to be followed by the pumping of water from the James River into the city, with the intent of drowning out the Confederates. Grant's staff officer Horace Porter recalled that another would-be strategist had developed "an all-powerful snuff" that he recommended be loaded into artillery shells and exploded over Rebel entrenchments. The southerners would "be seized with such violent fits of sneezing that they would soon become physically exhausted . . . and the Union army could walk over at its leisure." In response,

Grant deadpanned, "This is a very suggestive age." "In the end," he continued, "the only way to whip an army is to go out and fight it."[20]

Fighting Lee's army was exactly what Grant could not do at that moment. A man less disciplined might well have succumbed to his natural inclinations and attempted to force the issue with an all-out assault, but Grant recognized that the potential cost of such a decision outweighed uncertain benefits. As much as it gnawed at him, he would keep tightening the noose around Richmond and Petersburg, biding his time while Sherman burned through southern resources and morale in the Carolinas and Lee struggled to keep a patchwork defense of the Confederate capital from unraveling. In a telegram to Secretary of War Stanton, the commanding general admitted how difficult it was to restrain his natural aggressiveness in favor of a more prudent strategy, one that was the correct approach to defeating Lee, which was after all the ultimate objective. "I shall necessarily have to take the odium of apparent inactivity," he wrote on February 4, 1865, "but if it results, as I expect it will, in the discomfiture of Lee's Army, I shall be entirely satisfied."[21]

Grant soon found his expectations confirmed when in early March Lee sent a communiqué that suggested a turning point was imminent. Almost as an afterthought in a message about prisoners, Lee suggested a meeting between the two commanding generals to discuss "the possibility of arriving at a satisfactory adjustment of the present unhappy difficulties, . . . desiring to leave nothing untried which may put an end to the calamities of war." Was this a sign that Lee recognized the game was up? Was he looking to open surrender negotiations? Despite what must have been an overwhelming desire to respond immediately, Grant recognized that this was a matter for the eyes of his superiors in Washington, so he cabled the secretary of war for instructions. Six hours later came word from Stanton: "The President directs me to say . . . that he wishes you to have no conference with Gen. Lee unless it be for the capitulation of Lee's army. . . . [Y]ou are not to decide, discuss, or confer upon any political question: such questions the President holds in his own hands." Clear enough; Grant was to stick to military operations and leave the negotiations to the political leaders, but, in the meantime, Stanton directed, "You are to press to the utmost, your military advantages." This suited Grant just fine as it allowed him to concentrate on what he did best, fighting the enemy. "I can assure you," he replied to Stanton's directive, "that no act of the enemy will prevent me pressing all advantages gained to the utmost of my ability. Neither will I under any circumstances exceed my authority or in any way embarrass the Govt." To Lee, Grant explained, "I have no authority to accede to your proposition for a conference on the subject proposed." However, should the general wish to discuss matters "purely of a military character," a meeting could be arranged. Lee proved unreceptive, at least for the moment, to Grant's counterinvitation, but for the Federal commander this curious correspondence suggested that the Confederates were beginning to feel "discomfiture."[22]

Over the next week or so, there were further signs that the Confederates were slipping toward crisis. It appeared that preparations were being made to abandon the entrenchments for a move west, perhaps toward Lynchburg, Virginia. Grant told Meade to have the army ready to move at "the very shortest possible notice, in case the enemy should evacuate or partially evacuate Petersburg." Sherman telegraphed from North Carolina suggesting that Grant might forgo initiating any major operations until Sherman's forces could be brought north for a final, overwhelming blow. But Grant would countenance no delays. From the bloody Overland campaign through the irritations of Petersburg's trenches, the cost had been too high to allow the wily Lee any chance to escape and make his way south, where he could extend the war for months. No, the matter must end here, and it must end soon.[23]

Grant reiterated his determination to end the war in Virginia at an extraordinary meeting of the Union high command that took place on March 28, 1865, aboard the steamboat *River Queen* on the James River. The president, who a few days earlier had made his way to Grant's headquarters at City Point, discussed strategy with Grant, Sherman, and Adm. David D. Porter, giving voice to his concerns that Lee might escape to the Carolinas or that the Confederates might strike a severe blow in North Carolina while Sherman was away from the front. Sherman reassured the president that the generals he had left in charge were quite capable and that he would be making his return as soon as the meeting had adjourned. Grant also did what he could to relieve Lincoln's anxiety by revealing to the president that the Army of the Potomac was poised to launch a major offensive the next day. Grant hoped it would be the last offensive of the war.[24]

In the days preceding the *River Queen* meeting, deserters from Lee's ranks had revealed that the Confederates were making preparations for a move. To where they could not say, but rations had been issued for a number of days, a sure sign of an imminent march. Grant decided that it was time to strike; his orders to Meade directed Federal troops to swing to the west and hit Lee's right flank, looking to cut the last rail lines going into Petersburg, thereby forcing Lee to either flee his entrenchments or hold them and starve. The Yankees who did not join in the attack would maintain their positions, remaining vigilant for any sign of weakening in their front; but Grant, perhaps haunted by visions of Cold Harbor, made clear that it was "not the intention to attack the enemy in his intrenched [*sic*] position but to force him out." If the Confederates did emerge from the trenches, he instructed, "Move in with your entire force."[25]

The final confrontation between Grant and Lee began the morning of March 29, 1865, with Sheridan's cavalry taking the lead. Early reports from the front were promising, with advances made along the length of the line. Encouraged, Grant pushed Sheridan to catch hold of every opportunity offered: "I now feel like ending the matter. . . . In the morning push round the enemy if you can and get on to his right rear. . . . We will act altogether as one Army here until it is seen what can be done with the enemy." The next morning, Sheridan was nearly giddy over the previous day's advances, boasting, "I can drive in the whole cavalry force of the enemy with ease." If given infantry support, he promised to crush Lee's flank. "I tell you," he went on with erupting enthusiasm, "I'm ready to strike out tomorrow and go to smashing things." Not everyone at Union headquarters shared the cavalry commander's supreme confidence as some worried that Joe

Johnston would break away from Sherman in the Carolinas and suddenly appear on the Virginia front to reinforce Lee. Grant replied in his now familiar understated earnestness that he would simply "crush [Johnston], and then go after Lee."[26]

Over the next few days, as March turned to April, Grant continued to press his officers to maintain a tight hold on the Confederates. On April 1, Grant informed Meade that Sheridan had "captured every thing before him" and that it was vital that corps commanders should "push now or everything will leave [their] front and be concentrated against Sheridan." They should "feel for a chance to get through the enemy's lines at once and if they can get through should push on tonight." When Meade speculated that the next step would be to pursue Lee as he fled Petersburg, Grant checked him, making clear, "We did not want to follow him; we wanted to get ahead of him and cut him off." Horatio Wright, the commander of the Sixth Corps, embraced the intent and spirit of Grant's directive, promising, "The Corps will go in solid and I am sure will make the 'Fur Fly.' . . . I expect we will have broken through the Rebel lines in fifteen minutes from the word go."[27]

Sheridan did indeed achieve considerable success on April 1 at the Battle of Five Forks, a devastating blow to Lee during the course of which he lost over five thousand men, compared to less than seven hundred Federals. Early on April 2, with so many of his soldiers gone and the last rail line severed, Lee saw that time was running short. He notified Jefferson Davis, "[There is] no prospect of doing more than holding our position here till night. I am not certain that I can do that. If I can I shall withdraw tonight north of the Appomattox. I advise that all preparations be made for leaving Richmond tonight." On the other side of the line, Lee's counterpart had moved forward to see for himself how close the Rebels might be to breaking when Confederate artillery fire began landing close enough that nervous staff officers suggested that relocation might be in order. "Well," Grant conceded, "they do seem to have the range on us." What he had seen in those brief moments, coupled with reports coming in from commanders all along the line, convinced him that the Confederates were beginning the long-anticipated breakout to the west. To Sheridan, who was still harassing Lee's right flank, Grant telegraphed, "I think nothing now is wanting but the approach of your force from the West to finish up the job." That evening, the evacuation was confirmed, and the hunt was on.[28]

The next day, April 3, Grant sent word to Meade to get the Army of the Potomac moving west along the Appomattox River in pursuit of the bolting Rebels. He admonished corps commanders to press the attack as vigorously as possible, unnecessarily reminding Sheridan, "The first object of present movement will be to intercept Lee's Army." He took a moment later in the day to share the good news with Sherman that both Petersburg and Richmond had fallen and that five corps and Sheridan's cavalry had taken up the chase. "This Army has now won a most decisive Victory and followed the enemy," he wrote, betraying the pride he felt in an army that had long suffered from poor confidence and worse leadership. They had finally bested Lee and equaled the fighting prowess of Grant's tough westerners, the Army of the Tennessee. Winning, Grant concluded, "is all that [the army] ever wanted to make it as good an Army as ever fought a battle."[29]

Richmond was at long last in Union hands, but, although the Army of Northern Virginia had abandoned the Confederate capital, they had also dodged the blow Grant had hoped to inflict and were instead in flight to the west. For both armies, the fourth day of April was given over to maneuver, the instinct to survive driving one, the anticipation of victory pulling the other. Orders circulated among the bluecoats to "press on making as long a march today as possible," to which the men in the ranks readily complied because, as Grant recalled, "they preferred marching without rations to running a possible risk of letting the enemy elude them." Horace Porter's assessment was that the troops realized "that this campaign was to be won by legs; that the great walking-match had begun."[30]

The next day, Sheridan reported from the west that the pursuit was becoming a rout. "*Everything*," he told Grant, "should be hurried forward with the utmost speed." Neither Grant nor his commanders needed encouragement. In the spring of 1864, when Grant was preparing the Army of the Potomac for the Overland campaign,

he had instructed General Meade that Lee's army was to be the target. Eleven months later, his orders to Meade had not changed:
"Lee's Army is the objective point and to capture that is all we want."
Through the Battles of the Wilderness and Spotsylvania, Cold Harbor and the Petersburg siege, Grant had concentrated his energies
and those of the army on the war's true center of gravity, and now
that focus and patience were about to pay dividends. To Sherman in
North Carolina went the same message: "Push on from where you
are, and let us see if we cannot finish the job with Lee's and Johnston's armies. . . . Rebel armies now are the only strategic points to
strike at." From the general-in-chief to the men in the ranks, there
was a breathless anticipation that the war's end was fast approaching.
One soldier said after seeing Grant ride by, "The rebs are going to
get busted tomorrow, certain." "The troops," Grant observed, "are
all pushing now though it is after night and they have had no rest for
more than one week. The finest spirits prevails [*sic*] among the men
and I believe that in three days more Lee will not have an army."[31]

As telegrams from the front filtered into the War Department
in Washington, expectations among Lincoln and his war cabinet began to rise as well. On April 6, Grant forwarded to the president
a report from Sheridan that recounted his most recent action, including the capture of one of Lee's most senior corps commanders,
Richard Ewell, and Lee's eldest son, Custis Lee. Sheridan concluded
with the assessment, "If the thing is pressed, I think that Lee will surrender." The next morning brought Lincoln's reply: "Let the *thing*
be pressed." Grant got off another cable to Sherman, nearly identical
to that of the previous day, showing his mounting excitement and
anticipation: "I shall press the pursuit to the end. Push Johnston at
the same time and let us finish up this job all at once." Later that
afternoon, after assessing further news from his corps commanders,
including the now prisoner of war Richard Ewell's admission that
the war was for all intents and purposes over, Grant called for pen
and paper and with a steady hand composed a message addressed to
"Gen. R. E. Lee, Commanding": "The result of the last week must
convince you of the hopelessness of further resistance. . . . I feel that

it is so and regard it as my duty to shift from myself, the responsibility of any further effusion of blood by asking of you the surrender of . . . the Army of Northern Va." Lee received the note with Gen. James Longstreet, his "old war horse," by his side, who told Lee, "Not yet." Then followed an exchange of messages that shortly brought together the two war chiefs on April 9, in Wilmer McLean's front parlor in the tiny Virginia crossroads village of Appomattox Court House. It comes as no surprise that to the last Grant refused to loosen his grip, telling Sheridan on the eighth, "We will push him until terms are agreed upon," and telegraphing Secretary of War Stanton the morning of April 9, "There has been no relaxation in the pursuit during [the exchange of messages]."[32]

The terms agreed on in the McLean home reflected Grant's respect for Lee, a fellow officer whose sense of duty had required him to serve a different cause, and his recognition of the Confederate army's debilitated condition. At the same time, and more important, Grant understood his president's wishes, which accorded with his own, for lenient terms that would as rapidly as possible bring the southern soldier to exchange his rifle for a plow. All military goods would be confiscated; the men were to be paroled, allowing them to return home on their promise not to participate again in the war until exchanged for a Union prisoner; officers were permitted to keep their sidearms; any man who owned a horse or mule would be allowed to take the animal to begin spring planting; and, finally, Grant gave assurance that the men would not "be disturbed by United States Authority so long as they observe their parole and the laws in force where they may reside." Grant likely exceeded his authority as military commander with this last clause, but it fulfilled Lincoln's hopes to begin reconstruction and reconciliation as soon as possible. At 4:30 in the afternoon on April 9, Palm Sunday, Grant wired Secretary Stanton from the front, "Gen. Lee surrendered the Army of Northern Va. this afternoon on terms proposed by myself." That evening came Stanton's reply, expressing the thoughts of a nation nearly spent after four years of war, "Thanks be to Almighty God."[33]

With Lee's surrender secured, Grant stood in McLean's front

yard and watched as the Confederate commander departed for his troops, carrying the news that for them the war had come to an end. The elation the Union commander might have anticipated did not come, but rather his mood was "sad and depressed," which accounts for his orders to withhold any signs of celebration. "The war is over," he told his officers, "the rebels are our countrymen again." Throughout the war, a relentless pursuit of the enemy and victory had marked Grant's leadership, but now, at this moment of ultimate victory, he did not allow resentment or a desire for retribution to taint the accomplishments that he and the Union cause had achieved. His professionalism, integrity, and respect for an honorable enemy would countenance nothing less.[34]

The war, however, was not over, and for a number of weeks Grant continued to oversee ongoing Federal operations. To Gen. John Pope in St. Louis, he sent orders to prepare for a campaign against the Confederate Edmund Kirby Smith if Smith failed to respond affirmatively to a demand of surrender. To Gen. Edward Canby, who had just captured Mobile, Alabama, Grant gave the new objective of Texas, with directions to "commence operations immediately" against Galveston and to expect a cooperative attack by Union forces from Arkansas. By getting Sheridan's cavalry on the road south, he also looked to speed along the surrender of the largest remaining Confederate force, Joseph Johnston's army, which was dodging Sherman in North Carolina. Any worries he might have held about the Carolina operation proved unfounded; Sherman sent word on April 18 that Johnston had agreed to a surrender that Sherman believed would "produce Peace from the Potomac to the Rio Grand [*sic*]." It would take a little more negotiating, not only with Johnston, but also with the Lincoln administration, to finalize the terms, but within a few days the Confederate army in North Carolina had laid down its arms, and over the following weeks others would do likewise. The war was now fully, finally, over.[35]

Writing to a friend on April 17, 1865, the commanding general acknowledged the pressures of four years of war, confessing, "I would enjoy a little respite from my cares and responsibilities more than you can conceive." But the tragic events that occurred three days earlier disabused Grant of any idea of a reprieve from the strains of command. Early in the day on April 14, Grant attended a meeting with the president and cabinet members to further outline reconstruction policies for the seceded state governments. After declining an invitation to join the president and first lady that evening at the theater, Grant excused himself and headed for the train station, where he, Julia, and their son Jesse boarded a train for Philadelphia. They arrived not long after midnight. Once at their hotel, Grant found a telegram waiting for him from the War Department: "The President was assassinated at Fords [sic] Theatre at 10:30 tonight and cannot live. The wound is a Pistol shot through the head. Secretary [of State] Seward and his son Frederick, were also assassinated at their residence and are in a dangerous condition. The Secretary of War desires that you return to Washington immediately."[36]

After getting Julia and Jesse settled in the hotel, Grant set out for the capital with the heaviest of hearts. He later recalled, "It was the darkest day of my life." Thus, there would be no rest for the general-in-chief as the government, with the moderating restraint of Lincoln's guiding hand gone, would now more than ever have need of his steady and clear-headed determination. There was much work yet to be done.[37]

8

A Faith in Success

I believe determination can do a great deal to sustain one.

—Ulysses S. Grant

The spring of 1865 reached full bloom in late April and early May. During this traditional time of renewal and rebirth, northerners rightly expected to be in full-throated celebration of war's end, but instead they wore the black of mourning for their fallen president. With Father Abraham gone—"Now he belongs to the ages," Secretary of War Stanton eulogized at Lincoln's deathbed—the country instinctively looked to Grant, the man who had earned the nation's trust and confidence by first earning that of the now dead president. Indeed, Grant had succeeded where a roll call of generals had failed, men whose military training, experience in the field, and even charisma all suggested that they should have worn the victor's wreath, not the diminutive, taciturn westerner who a friend said "could remain silent in several languages." How could this man with a perpetually rumpled coat and reputation for drink, who did not look or act the part of a great warrior like a George McClellan was wont to do, win the war? Acknowledging that the causative factors for any historical event are complex beyond ready explanation, the paramount reason for Grant's overwhelming success as a military commander, and thus by extension the Union's ultimate victory, was his analytical determination.[1]

Over the years, historians and others have offered alternative explanations for Grant's success, some appearing almost before the ink of Lee's signature at Appomattox had dried. A few of these arguments are persuasive and therefore worthy of consideration. The long-acknowledged maxim that "God favors the biggest battalions" at first glance seems obvious and beyond challenge. Nevertheless, all Americans, including Grant and his contemporaries, know of the Americans' unlikely victory over the British in the Revolution. More recent memory provides the cautionary tale of the twentieth century's industrial and economic American Goliath being checked, if not slain, by the David of North Vietnam. Such exceptions aside, typically the combatant who marshals the largest battalions and greater resources enjoys the best chance of success, and such was the case for Grant in the Civil War. From a strategic perspective, the United States maintained an overwhelming advantage throughout the war in both manpower and industrial capacity, the details of which are so familiar that repetition here is unnecessary. At the operational and tactical level, in almost every instance Grant's combat power equaled or surpassed that of his opponent, with the notable exception of the Vicksburg campaign, where poor Confederate leadership negated a southern numerical advantage. Clearly, Grant won in the end because of overwhelming resources. But is it that simple?

To attribute Grant's success exclusively or even primarily to this wealth of resources is to ignore his record and the record of his predecessors in high command. In his first major battles at Forts Henry and Donelson, Union and Confederate forces in the region were appreciably the same, both in number and in experience. Lincoln's observation to Irwin McDowell in the summer of 1861, "You are green, it is true; but they are green also; you are all green alike," is equally applicable to the war's western theater in the spring of 1862. A few months after Donelson at Shiloh, on the battle's first day both armies mustered about forty thousand, and, while some credit the timely arrival of the Army of the Ohio with saving Grant's command, Grant maintained and the evidence suggests that, with the appearance of Lew Wallace's division from his own Army of the Tennessee, Grant would likely have achieved the same outcome against an exhausted and spent Confederate foe.[2]

The Overland campaign two years later against Robert E. Lee is perhaps the most frequently cited instance where the Union advantage in manpower and material was the deciding factor, and there is no denying that if Grant had not enjoyed such an advantage in resources his generalship would have been sorely tested against such a shrewd and capable opponent. Nevertheless, the point here is to compare, not Grant to Lee, but Grant to his predecessors in command of the Army of the Potomac, all of whom enjoyed an equal, if not greater, material advantage over Lee as did Grant, yet not one of whom proved up to the task of defeating the Confederate Grey Fox. George McClellan, John Pope, McClellan again, Ambrose Burnside, Joe Hooker, and George Meade all had at their disposal an army that surpassed that of their opponent in every measurable way; nevertheless, in the intangible of leadership each faltered. Each commander in his own way lacked the analytical determination necessary to transform his wealth of resources into a battlefield victory that would decisively alter the course of the war. During the Peninsula campaign of 1862, with his army poised on the outskirts of Richmond, McClellan surrendered to his inner doubts and ordered a retreat, revealing a lack of confidence that he again displayed at Antietam just a few months later. There he let slip away an opportunity to annihilate Lee's army, a failure that led to his removal from command. Ambrose Burnside, unlike the others, did demonstrate a high degree of perseverance at the Battle of Fredericksburg in late 1862; unfortunately, his resolve was of the obtuse, stubborn variety that sent wave after forlorn wave of Union infantry against the impregnable Confederate earthworks on Marye's Heights. He achieved nothing more than the loss of many a good soldier. At the Battle of Chancellorsville in May 1863, Joe Hooker lost his nerve despite outnumbering Lee more than two to one, a lapse Hooker later explained with the awkwardly honest self-assessment, "I lost confidence in Joe Hooker."[3] Of all those who commanded the Army of the Potomac, only Grant exercised a determination tempered by thoughtful reasoning to make effective use of his advantage in men and material.

Another explanation for Grant's success is that he enjoyed the good fortune of beginning the war in relative obscurity, both in reputation and in location. Far from the political intrigues of Washington and the unforgiving scrutiny of the press, he commanded a regiment of infantry volunteers in the backwaters of Illinois and Missouri. Unlike officers in the East, he was afforded an anonymity that gave him time to learn his trade by trial and error and mature as a leader without the expectation of immediate and spectacular success. Unquestionably, Grant grew into the job, learning from his mistakes and mentors like Charles F. Smith, and had he been immediately thrust into the lead role of commanding the Army of the Potomac he might have failed miserably. Yet he was not unique among Union officers in having an opportunity to become acclimated to the responsibilities of high command. Prior to his appointment to lead the Army of the Potomac in 1861, George McClellan had conducted operations in western Virginia, where at Philippi and Rich Mountain he won fame as the "Young Napoléon." Even after the disaster of the Peninsula campaign, made all the worse by McClellan condemning President Lincoln and Secretary of War Stanton for his own shortcomings, he retained command of the army. Then, in a fantastic demonstration of lessons not learned, he again managed through a deficiency of nerve and determination to allow Lee's army to escape at Antietam. Those who followed Little Mac in command turned in performances that were at best a marginal improvement, despite the fact that by the time they were elevated to lead the army all had gained considerable experience as division and corps commanders, off center stage and with the chance to learn from experience and senior officers. John Pope, Ambrose Burnside, Joe Hooker, and even to some degree George Meade either failed to take advantage of the opportunities division and corps command offered to develop their own abilities or had been elevated beyond the highest level of their competency. While Grant did indeed benefit from being off center stage in the West, so too did other senior commanders have an opportunity to refine their leadership skills before being blessed—or cursed—as commander of the Army of the Potomac. Thus, attributing Grant's success to either a preponderance of resources or having enjoyed a grace period denied other commanders is unconvincing and does not account for his extraordinary leadership and war record.

Another criticism lodged against Grant is that he cavalierly sacrificed the lives of his men to achieve victory at too high a cost. More to the point, he has been stamped a butcher who showed a disregard for casualties and little concern for the welfare of his men, being all too ready to order a quick and bloody frontal assault, either too callous or too slow-witted to consider alternatives. Perhaps most famously Mary Lincoln, on reading of the losses incurred during the Overland campaign, bitterly complained to her husband that Grant was "a butcher": "He loses two men to the enemy's one. He has no management, no regard for life. . . . According to his tactics, there is nothing under the heavens to do but march a new line of men up in front of the rebel breastworks to be shot down as fast as they take their position, and keep marching until the enemy grows tired of the slaughter. Grant, I repeat, is an obstinate fool and a butcher." When one looks at the number of casualties the Union Army suffered during those four grim weeks in May 1864, one is inclined to agree with Mrs. Lincoln, but a closer examination suggests that she was unfairly harsh on the general-in-chief.[4]

Edward H. Bonekemper's *A Victor, Not a Butcher* exhaustively examines this issue, and his findings reveal that among Civil War commanders Grant was far from the most accomplished of the "butchers." During the horrific Overland campaign, Federal forces suffered casualties of 34 percent, while Lee's Confederates, who in most engagements fought on the defensive and therefore were likely to suffer fewer dead and wounded, suffered casualties of 43 percent. For the entire war, Grant's casualty rate of 15 percent compares quite favorably with Lee's 20.2 percent, an advantage Grant also maintained over other Confederate commanders such as Braxton Bragg (19.5 percent), John B. Hood (19.2 percent), and P. G. T. Beauregard (16.1 percent). Given that Union forces typically outnumbered their Confederate opponents, one might expect that, although Grant's percentage of casualties was lower, in sheer numbers he would have a longer casualty list. Bonekemper's findings, however, reveal that from the Battle of Belmont in November 1861 to the conclusion of the war, Grant's commands inflicted 190,760 casualties on southern forces while suffering 153,642, a difference of 37,118 more Confederate casualties.[5]

Grant's approach to war fighting, both in statement and in practice, has contributed to this characterization of unthinking aggressiveness. At Fort Donelson in February 1862, he first came to the realization that the commander who seizes the initiative and presses the attack is most likely to win, a philosophy that informed his decisionmaking throughout the war and culminated in the lengthy casualty lists of the Overland campaign. His philosophy, however, was more refined and sophisticated than this might suggest. Recall that soon after the victory at Fort Donelson he told wife Julia, "I want to push on as rapidly as possible to save hard fighting. These terrible battles are very good things to read about for persons who loose no friends but I am decidedly in favor of having as little of it as possible. *The way to avoid it is to push forward as vigorously as possible.*" Far better, Grant believed, to suffer casualties now and end the war sooner than to avoid battle in the false hope that the war would conclude later without hard fighting and fewer casualties. Locked in battle with Lee in 1864, he knew that he could, as his aide Horace Porter recounted, "avoid all bloodshed by remaining north of the Rapidan, entrenching, and not moving against his enemy," but, after three years of war, he understood that "peace could be secured only by whipping and destroying the enemy, . . . that in campaigning the hardest blows bring the quickest relief."[6]

Grant also knew that the destruction of the enemy could be achieved in a variety of ways, and despite what his critics contend he seldom turned first to the blunt hammer of a frontal assault. The Vicksburg campaign more than any other demonstrates that his commitment to offensive operations was predicated on outmaneuvering his enemy. After his initial attempts to reach Vicksburg failed, all of which were designed to reach the city by an indirect route, Grant worked with Admiral Porter to orchestrate the river crossing that brought his army to within a day's march of the town. Eschewing the most direct and therefore most obvious path to Vicksburg, he instead turned northeast, drove to Jackson, and scattered Joe Johnston's gathering force before striking toward Vicksburg, along the way winning four battles in five days while befuddling the enemy as to his next move. When he arrived at Vicksburg, he twice ordered attacks in the expectation of taking the city before the southerners could fully develop their entrenchments, but on successive failures he recognized that further assaults would gain little for the likely cost. He then wisely chose the more conservative strategy of siege operations.

The same reliance on maneuver over direct assault characterized Grant's succeeding campaigns at Chattanooga and in Virginia. Recall that the astounding charge up Missionary Ridge at Chattanooga surprised no one more than Grant, who had designated Sherman's corps on the Union left flank as the main assault, with Joe Hooker's force on the right in support. As for the Overland campaign, Grant's strategy was simple enough: the objective was to destroy Lee's army before it could withdraw to the defenses of Richmond, and this could best be accomplished by catching the Confederates in the open, or as Grant said, "It was better to fight him outside of his stronghold than in it." With each engagement from the Wilderness to Cold Harbor, Grant anticipated overtaking the Confederates before they could entrench, but in each instance Lee deftly parried the Union thrust. Like two wrestlers, each army worked to gain an advantage over the other, and after each move the Yankees tested the resolve of the southerners and the strength of their position, as at the Mule Shoe near Spotsylvania. Failing to gain a decisive advantage, Grant repeatedly maneuvered to his left, looking to avoid an assault against impenetrable earthworks. That May, Charles Dana reported from the front, "If a promising chance offers, General Grant will fight, of course; otherwise, he will maneuver without attacking." Time and again, Grant probed the Confederate flank for an opportune gap or, less likely, a mistake by Lee. It was Grant, however, who made the most costly mistake of the campaign with his decision to charge the Confederates at Cold Harbor, a grand error in judgment that he immediately recognized and acknowledged and for which he assumed full responsibility. Then, as at Vicksburg, with the southerners holed up in their fortifications around Richmond and Petersburg, he avoided further frontal assaults that promised little success in favor of the ennui of siege operations that traded immediate results for conservation of men and material. So, despite the significant number of casualties suffered by his armies over the course of the war, Grant hardly deserves condemnation as a butcher. But myths die hard. Those who will continue to pass such judgment on him should first call other commanders out of the historical shadows to accept responsibility for their higher contribution to the war's body count.[7]

Those who best knew Grant during the war, his staff and fellow officers, would have found little in Mary Lincoln's assessment with which they would have agreed, especially her implication that he lacked compassion or integrity. Horace Porter, who served as an aide to Grant in the latter half of the war, observed his concern for the daily well-being of his men, his concern for the wounded, who "visibly affected" him, and his pleasure in high prisoner counts as he believed "it was always more humane to reduce the enemy's strength by captures than by slaughter." Grant's empathy even extended to animals; he described the bullfights he witnessed during the Mexican War as "sickening": "I could not see how human beings could enjoy the sufferings of beasts." And he once took a teamster to task for severely beating a horse.[8]

Likely owing to his reputation for drinking, historians have often overlooked or ignored Grant's high sense of honor and integrity. Nearly all who knew him acknowledged that Grant recognized the inherent dignity of every man, including, significantly, himself. It comes as no surprise that Sherman was effusive in his praise for his captain, comparing him favorably to Washington, "as unselfish, kind-hearted, and honest, as a man should be." Horace Porter recalled that Grant "never underrated himself in a battle; he never overrated himself in a report"; the staff officer Rufus Ingalls described him as the "most absolutely truthful person" he knew; another aide agreed that he was "tediously truthful." Perhaps a more objective assessment came from the newspaper man Sylvanus Cadwallader, who concisely stated, "He was honest," and recorded Grant's distaste for off-color jokes and stories along with his aversion to swearing, although Grant did confess that he "would have the charity to excuse those who may have [used profanity], if they were in charge of a train of Mexican pack mules."[9]

Grant's Confederate opponents provide further testament to his integrity. Simon Bolivar Buckner, the commander of Fort Donelson in February 1862 and the unfortunate recipient of Grant's first "unconditional surrender" demand, recalled that after the surrender was finalized Grant followed him to a private room, where in "that modest manner peculiar to himself . . . [he] tendered me his purse" as repayment for a kindness Buckner had offered during Grant's difficult times before the war. Gen. James Longstreet, who thought Grant "the soul of honor" when they wore the cadet gray of West Point, told the story related in a previous chapter of Grant stopping him on a street in St. Louis in the prewar years to repay a fifteen-year-old debt even though it was apparent to Longstreet that Grant had fallen on hard times. While Grant would become best known as a fighter, Longstreet maintained that "the biggest part of him was his heart."[10]

In December of 1864, a time of mixed emotions, with jubilation over Sherman's capture of Savannah tempered by the tedium of the Petersburg siege, Grant sought to reassure his wife, Julia, of his well-being and in doing so identified his greatest strength: "I believe determination can do a great deal to sustain one and I have that quality certainly to its fullest extent." A few months earlier, Sherman had reached the same conclusion, telling Grant, "The chief characteristic in your nature is the simple faith in success you have always manifested."[11]

It is worth revisiting Carl von Clausewitz's observations on the essential quality of leadership:

> As soon as difficulties arise—and that must always happen when great results are at stake . . . the Commander must have a great force of will. . . . As the forces in one individual after another become prostrated, and can no longer be excited and supported by an effort of his own will, the whole inertia of the mass gradually rests its weight on the Will of

the Commander: by the spark in his breast, by the light of
his spirit, the spark of purpose, the light of hope, must be
kindled afresh in others: in so far only as he is equal to this,
he stands above the masses and continues to be their master.

Horace Porter's description of Grant presents his commander as the
personification of Clausewitz's ideal leader: "always calm amid excitement, and patient under trials. He looked neither to the past with
regret nor to the future with apprehension. When he could not control he endured, and in every great crisis he could 'convince when
others could not advise.' His calmness of demeanor and unruffled
temper were often a marvel even to those most familiar with him. In
the midst of the most exciting scenes he rarely raised his voice above
its ordinary pitch or manifested the least irritability." Grant demonstrated the ability to assess the situation and make the necessary adap-
tations, all while keeping a level head. Clausewitz would have simply
said that Grant possessed a "great force of will."[12]

William T. Sherman once observed of Grant, "To me he is a mystery, and I believe he is a mystery to himself." Nevertheless, as in-
scrutable as Grant might have been even to Sherman, a study of his
life and campaigns reveals the explanation for his success. What made
Grant effective was that each decision was, not an end in itself, but
a stepping stone toward achieving an ultimate objective, from the
capture of Vicksburg, to regaining the initiative at Chattanooga, to
the destruction of Lee's army, to final victory. Grant's success came
from his ability to identify a campaign's proper objective and then
permit nothing to distract or dissuade him from the pursuit of that
objective, and, while he possessed many of the qualities of successful
leadership, his analytical determination is the principal explanation
for why Ulysses S. Grant won the Civil War.[13]

Acknowledgments

The writing of this book would not have been possible without the help of a number of people. Jeffrey Matthews of the University of Puget Sound read, reread, and then read again every paragraph of the manuscript, providing invaluable advice and encouragement when it was most needed. William Robison, the head of the Department of History and Political Science, Southeastern Louisiana University, consistently put together a class schedule that allowed me time to be both a teacher and a historian. Stephen Wrinn, the director of the University Press of Kentucky, gave his support to this project when it was absolutely essential. He and his staff of professionals have once again made the publishing process a pleasure rather than an ordeal. The Press's anonymous readers provided honest and pointed critiques, all of which significantly improved the manuscript's final version. I would also like to thank those who over the years shared the pleasures and camaraderie of walking battlefields such as Shiloh, Vicksburg, Gettysburg, Vimy, and Normandy. The forests, fields, and beaches that once heard the din of battle now eavesdrop on the quiet musings of the dearest of friends. Finally, to Tara, my wife and best friend, my thanks for keeping me ever mindful that life is about the present and not the past.

Notes

The following abbreviations have been used throughout the notes:

OR   *War of the Rebellion*
PUSG Simon, ed., *Papers of Ulysses S. Grant.*

Introduction

1. Grant quoted in Catton, *Grant Moves South,* 223; Daniel, *Shiloh,* 173–76.
2. Johnston quoted in Cunningham, *Shiloh and the Western Campaign,* 138.
3. Grant quoted in "Report of Brig. Gen. B. M. Prentiss, U.S. Army, Commanding Sixth Division," November 17, 1862, in *OR,* ser. 1, 10, pt. 1:278–79.
4. Simpson, *Ulysses S. Grant,* 130; Sword, *Shiloh,* 107–18, 352–53; Smith, *Grant,* 201.
5. Wong, Bliese, and McGurk, "Military Leadership," 669. See also Reed, Bullis, Collins, and Paprone, "Mapping the Route of Leadership Education."
6. Clausewitz, *On War,* 145, 141–44.
7. Clausewitz, *On War,* 143 (emphasis added).
8. For a thorough analysis of the "Grant as butcher" argument, see Bonekemper, *A Victor, Not a Butcher.* For a review of historiography on the butcher thesis, see ibid., xi–xviii.
9. McFeely, *Grant,* 165; Simpson, *Ulysses S. Grant;* Smith, *Grant;* Waugh, *U. S. Grant.* The historiography of Grant is extensive, if not in fact overwhelming. Fortunately for Grant scholars, Ethan S. Rafuse published a fine historiographic essay, "Still a Mystery?" that effectively reviews the significant literature of the last twenty-five years.
10. For examples of books on corporate leadership, see Isaacson, *Steve Jobs;* Schultz and Gordon, *Onward;* and Branson, *Losing My Virginity.* The beginning source for battlefield staff rides is Robertson, *The Staff Ride.* Guidebooks based on the staff ride model exist for nearly every battlefield. See, e.g., Luvaas, Bowman, and Fullenkamp, eds., *Guide to the Battle of Shiloh;* and Grimsley and Woodworth, *Shiloh.*

11. Slim quoted in Tsouras, ed., *The Book of Military Quotations*, 249.

1. First Lessons

1. Simpson, *Ulysses S. Grant*, 2–7; Grant, *Memoirs*, 1:26; Waugh, *U. S. Grant*, 13–20.
2. Grant, *Memoirs*, 1:28.
3. Ibid., 31–33; Simpson, *Ulysses S. Grant*, 9–17; Smith, *Grant*, 23–28.
4. Interview with Lafayette McLaws, *New York Times*, July 24, 1885, 6 (col. 7); Smith, *Grant*, 40.
5. Grant, *Memoirs*, 1:69. For more on Taylor, see Bauer, *Zachary Taylor.*
6. Grant, *Memoirs*, 1:66.
7. Ibid., 94–95.
8. Wellington quoted in Millett and Maslowski, *For the Common Defense*, 156.
9. Grant, *Memoirs*, 1:89–95; Grant to unknown, August 22, 1847, in *PUSG*, 1:144.
10. Simpson, *Ulysses S. Grant*, 54–56; Smith, *Grant*, 78; Grant, *Memoirs*, 1:131–34.
11. Grant, *Memoirs*, 1:135–40; contractor quoted in Smith, *Grant*, 85.
12. Grant, *Memoirs*, 1:141–42; James Longstreet interview in the *New York Times*, July 24, 1885, quoted in Smith, *Grant*, 93; Simpson, *Ulysses S. Grant*, 63–77; Waugh, *U. S. Grant*, 47.
13. Grant, *Memoirs*, 1:142.

2. First Battles

1. Grant, *Memoirs*, 1:161–62; Smith, *Grant*, 107–8.
2. Grant, *Memoirs*, 1:162–63.
3. Ibid., 164.
4. Ibid., 56, 164–65.
5. Ibid., 174; Grant to Julia Grant, October 20, 1862, in *PUSG*, 3:63–64; Elihu B. Washburne to Salmon P. Chase, October 31, 1861, in ibid., 98; Hughes, *The Battle of Belmont*, 5.
6. Grant, *Memoirs*, 1:178. See also Grant's second report on the Battle of Belmont, in *PUSG*, 3:146; and Hughes, *The Battle of Belmont*, 51.
7. Grant, *Memoirs*, 1:178–80; Hughes, *The Battle of Belmont*, 121.
8. Grant, *Memoirs*, 1:180–83; Simpson, *Ulysses S. Grant*, 98–103; Smith, *Grant*, 125–24.
9. Grant, *Memoirs*, 1:180–83; Simpson, *Ulysses S. Grant*, 98–103; Smith, *Grant*, 125–24.
10. Grant to Charles F. Smith, November 8, 1861, in *PUSG*, 3:134; Grant to Seth Williams, November 10, 1861, in ibid., 141–42. Grant also

describes the victory as "complete" in letters to Chauncey McKeever, assistant adjutant general, Western Department, St. Louis (Grant to McKeever, November 8, 1861, in ibid., 133), and to his father (Grant to Jesse Grant, November 8, 1861, in ibid., 137–38).

11. Illinois soldier and Wallace quoted in Hughes, *The Battle of Belmont*, 134, 135.

12. Grant's second report on the Battle of Belmont, in *PUSG*, 3:149; Grant to Jesse Grant, November 8, 1861, in ibid., 138; John McClernand's report on the Battle of Belmont, in ibid., 197; Leonidas Polk to Francis D. Polk, November 15, 1861, quoted in Hughes, *The Battle of Belmont*, 187.

13. Fredriksen, ed., *American Military Leaders*, 1:311–12; Grant, *Memoirs*, 1:189; Henry Halleck to Grant, January 6, 1862, in *PUSG*, 4:4n; McPherson, *Tried by War*, 69.

14. There remains a question as to who actually first proposed the Fort Henry operation, Grant or Halleck. Grant argues that he first suggested the campaign to Halleck in early January. See Grant, *Memoirs*, 1:189–90. On January 6, 1862, Halleck did instruct Grant to carry out the demonstration noted above but made no mention of an operation to actually seize Fort Henry. Halleck informed Gen. George McClellan in Washington of the same on January 9. See Henry Halleck to Grant, January 6, 1862, in *PUSG*, 4:4n; and Henry Halleck to George McClellan, January 9, 1862, in *OR*, ser. 1, 7:539–40. Sherman believed that Halleck was the originator. See Sherman, *Memoirs*, 1:238. Foote gave the credit to Grant. See Foote to Grant, March 8, 1862, in *PUSG*, 4:314n. Two telegrams sent by Grant to Halleck in late January suggest that, if the initial idea was not Grant's, he provided the operational objectives and details. Grant to Halleck, January 28, 29, 1862, in ibid., 99, 103. See also Simpson, *Ulysses S. Grant*, 109–10. For the telegram exchange among Grant, Foote, and Halleck in which the decision is made to move against Fort Henry, see *OR*, ser. 1, 7:120–22.

15. Grant to Julia Grant, February 4, 1862, in *PUSG*, 4:149; Grant to Capt. John C. Kelton, February 6, 1862, in ibid., 157; Grant to Halleck, February 6, 1862, in *OR*, ser. 1, 7:124; Grant to Mary Grant, February 9, 1862, in *PUSG*, 4:179; Simpson, *Ulysses S. Grant*, 108–12; Smith, *Grant*, 139–47.

16. Grant to John McClernand, February 7, 1862, in *PUSG*, 4:165; Grant, *Memoirs*, 1:197; Grant to George W. Cullum, February 8, 1862, in *PUSG*, 4:171.

17. Lew Wallace, "The Capture of Fort Donelson," in Johnson and Buel, eds., *Battles and Leaders*, 1:422; Grant, *Memoirs*, 1:205, 208; Grant to Andrew Foote, February 15, 1862, in *PUSG*, 4:214; Simpson, *Ulysses S. Grant*, 113–18; Smith, *Grant*, 147–66.

18. Smith quoted in Simpson, *Ulysses S. Grant,* 117; Grant to Simon B. Buckner, February 16, 1862, in *PUSG,* 4:218; Buckner to Grant, February 16, 1862, in ibid., 218n; Grant to Henry Halleck, February 16, 1862, in *OR,* ser. 1, 7:625; Lincoln quoted in *PUSG,* 4:272; Simpson, *Ulysses S. Grant,* 45, 63.

19. Wallace, "The Capture of Fort Donelson," in Johnson and Buel, eds., *Battles and Leaders,* 1:422, 404; Simpson, *Ulysses S. Grant,* 113–18; Smith, *Grant,* 147–66; Waugh, *U. S. Grant,* 55.

20. Wallace, "The Capture of Fort Donelson," in Johnson and Buel, eds., *Battles and Leaders,* 1:405; Grant, *Memoirs,* 1:33, 221; Charles F. Smith to unknown, March 17, 1862, in *PUSG,* 4:344n; Grant to Elihu B. Washburne, February 10, 1862, in ibid., 188.

21. Smith quoted in Wallace, *An Autobiography,* 1:345; Grant on his philosophy of war quoted in Brinton, *Personal Memoirs,* 239; Smith, *Grant,* 208; Simpson, *Ulysses S. Grant,* 138.

22. Col. Cadwallader C. Washburn to Elihu B. Washburne, March 3, 1862, in *PUSG,* 4:307n; Grant to George W. Cullum, February 16, 1862, in ibid., 227; Grant to George W. Cullum, February 19, 1862, in ibid., 245; Grant to George W. Cullum, February 21, 1862, in ibid., 257; Andrew Foote to George W. Cullum, February 21, 1862, in *OR,* ser. 1, 7:648.

23. Henry Halleck to Thomas A. Scott, Assistant Secretary of War, February 21, 1862, in *OR,* ser. 1, 7:648; Henry Halleck to Grant, February 18, 1862, in *PUSG,* 4:259–60; Andrew Foote to Grant, February 22, 1862, in ibid., 262; Grant to Julia Grant, February 22, 1862, in ibid., 271; Grant to Julia Grant, March 1, 1862, in ibid., 305; Grant to Julia Grant, February 24, 1862, in ibid., 284.

24. Henry Halleck to George B. McClellan, March 3, 1862, in *OR,* ser. 1, 7:680; George B. McClellan to Henry Halleck, March 3, 1862, in ibid.; Henry Halleck to George B. McClellan, March 4, 1862, in ibid., 682; Henry Halleck to Grant, March 4, 1862, in *PUSG,* 4:319n1; Simpson, *Ulysses S. Grant,* 121–25; Smith, *Grant,* 172–77.

25. Grant to Charles F. Smith, March 5, 1862, in *OR,* ser. 1, 10, pt. 2:6. For Grant's self-defense, see Grant to Henry Halleck, March 5, 1862, in *PUSG,* 4:317–19; and Grant to Henry Halleck, March 7, 1862, in ibid., 331. See also Simpson, *Ulysses S. Grant,* 121–25; and Smith, *Grant,* 172–77.

26. Henry Halleck to Lorenzo Thomas, Adjutant General of the Army, March 15, 1862, in *OR,* ser. 1, 7:683–84; Simpson, *Ulysses S. Grant,* 121–25; Smith, *Grant,* 172–77.

27. John McClernand, W. H. L. Wallace, Leonard F. Ross, and eight other officers to Grant, March 9, 1862, in *PUSG,* 4:338n; presentation speech by Col. C. Carroll Marsh, March 10, 1862, in ibid., 376n.

3. Shiloh

1. Henry Halleck to Grant, March 1, 1862, in *PUSG*, 4:310n; Grant to Capt. Nathaniel H. McLean, Assistant Adjutant General, Department of the Mississippi, March 20, 1862, in ibid., 397; Grant to Charles F. Smith, March 23, 1862, in ibid., 411.

2. Grant to William T. Sherman, April 4, 1862, in ibid., 5:9; Grant to W. H. L. Wallace, April 4, 1862, in ibid., 12; Grant to Henry Halleck, April 5, 1862, in ibid., 14.

3. Smith, *Grant*, 193; Grant to Commanding Officer, Advance Forces (of Buell's army), April 6, 1862, in *PUSG*, 5:18; Sword, *Shiloh*, 368; Catton, *Grant Moves South*, 237–38.

4. Catton, *Grant Moves South*, 241.

5. Grant to Buell, April 7, 1862, in *PUSG*, 5:20–21; Sherman, *Memoirs*, 1:266; Grant to Capt. Nathaniel H. McLean, Assistant Adjutant General, Department of the Mississippi, April 9, 1862, in *PUSG*, 5:33; Grant, *Memoirs*, 1:235–38.

6. Don Carlos Buell, "Shiloh Reviewed," in Johnson and Buell, eds., *Battles and Leaders*, 1:536; Grant to Capt. Speed Butler, August 23, 1861, in *PUSG*, 2:131; Grant to George P. Ihrie, April 25, 1862, in ibid., 5:73–74. See also Grant to Jesse Grant, April 26, 1862, in ibid., 78.

7. Grant, *Memoirs*, 1:223–24.

8. Ibid., 234; Sherman, *Memoirs*, 1:266.

9. Grant to Julia Grant, April 15, 1862, in *PUSG*, 5:47; Grant to Julia Grant, May 13, 1862, in ibid., 118. See also Grant to Julia Grant, May 16, 1862, in ibid., 123.

10. Henry Halleck to his wife, April 14, 1862, in *PUSG*, 5:48n1; Grant to Henry Halleck, April 25, 1862, in ibid., 67; Henry Halleck to Grant, April 14, 1862, in ibid., 49n1; Capt. Nathaniel H. McLean, Assistant Adjutant General, Department of the Mississippi, to Grant, April 14, 1862, in ibid., 49n1.

11. Special Field Orders No. 35, April 30, 1862, in *OR*, ser. 1, 10, pt. 2:144; Grant to Henry Halleck, May 11, 1862, in *PUSG*, 5:114; Grant to Julia Grant, May 11, 1862, in ibid., 116.

12. Sherman, *Memoirs*, 1:275–76.

13. Special Field Orders No. 90, June 10, 1862, in *OR*, ser. 1, 10, pt. 2:288; William T. Sherman to Grant, June 6, 1862, in *PUSG*, 5:141n1; Elihu B. Washburne to Grant, July 25, 1862, in ibid., 226n.

14. General Order No. 62, July 15, 1862, in *PUSG*, 5:210. For an example of the continuing tension between Grant and Halleck, see Grant to Henry Halleck, June 29, 1862, in *PUSG*, 5:169–70; and Halleck to Grant,

July 3, 1862, in ibid., 170n. See also Smith, *Grant*, 206–16; Simpson, *Ulysses S. Grant*, 136–46.

15. Clausewitz, *On War*, 145.

16. Grant, *Memoirs*, 1:264. For correspondence between Grant and Halleck on force deployment, see Halleck to Grant, August 9, 1862, in *PUSG*, 5:277; Halleck to Grant, August 14, 1862, in ibid., 292, 293n; Grant to Halleck, August 16, 1862, in ibid., 296; and Grant to Halleck, September 10, 1862, in ibid., 6:31.

17. Grant to William S. Rosecrans, September 14, 1862, in *PUSG*, 6:38; Grant to Jesse Grant, September 17, 1862, in ibid., 61. See also Grant to Henry Halleck, September 16, 1862, in ibid., 46.

18. Grant to William S. Rosecrans, September 18, 1862, in ibid., 64; Simpson, *Ulysses S. Grant*, 151–54. See also Grant to Edward Ord, September 20, 1862, in *PUSG*, 6:68–69.

19. Grant to Henry Halleck, October 1, 1862, in *PUSG*, 6:96; Grant to William S. Rosecrans, October 2, 1862, in ibid., 99–100n1; Grant to William S. Rosecrans, October 3, 1862, in ibid., 107; Grant to Stephen Hurlbut, October 3, 1862, in ibid., 106; Grant to William S. Rosecrans, October 4, 1862, in ibid., 114; Grant to Henry Halleck, October 5, 1862, in ibid., 116–17. See also Grant to Stephen Hurlbut, October 4, 1862, in ibid., 112.

20. Grant to William S. Rosecrans, October 7, 1862, in ibid., 131; Grant to Henry Halleck, October 7, 1862, in ibid., 130; Henry Halleck to Grant, October 8, 1862, in ibid., 130n.

21. William S. Rosecrans to Grant, October 7, 1862 (two telegrams), in ibid., 131–32n; Simpson, *Ulysses S. Grant*, 154–55. See also a series of telegrams from Grant to Henry Halleck, October 8, 1862, in *PUSG*, 6:133–34; and Grant to William S. Rosecrans, October 8, 1862, in ibid., 138. On Rosecrans's transfer request, see ibid., 182n.

22. Grant to Col. John C. Kelton, "Report on the Battle of Corinth," October 20, 1862, in *PUSG*, 6:223–24; Maj. Gen. William S. Rosecrans, "The Battle of Corinth," in Johnson and Buell, eds., *Battles and Leaders*, 2:755–56; William S. Rosecrans to Grant, October 9, 1862, in *PUSG*, 6:142; Simpson, *Ulysses S. Grant*, 155; Smith, *Grant*, 218–19.

23. Such generosity of spirit, however, did not keep him from relieving Rosecrans of command a year later when the situation at Chattanooga, Tennessee, reached the point of crisis. For Rosecrans's replacement of Buell, see *PUSG*, 6:182n; and Grant, *Memoirs*, 1:280–82.

4. The Vicksburg Campaign

1. Grant to Henry Halleck, October 26, 1862 (two telegrams), in *PUSG*, 6:197, 199–200; Grant, *Memoirs*, 1:281; Davis quoted in Winschel, *Vicksburg*, 14.

2. Grant to Henry Halleck, November 2, 1862, in *PUSG*, 6:243; Grant to William T. Sherman, November 14, 1862, in ibid., 312.

3. Grant to Benjamin Grierson, December 23, 1862, in ibid., 7:96.

4. Simpson, *Ulysses S. Grant*, 173–74; Grant to Julia Grant, February 14, 1863, in *PUSG*, 7:325; Grant to Henry Halleck, January 9, 1863, in ibid., 204; Grant, *Memoirs*, 1:296.

5. Grant to John McClernand, January 10, 1863, in *PUSG*, 7:207; Grant to Willis A. Gorman, January 22, 1863, in ibid., 242–43; Grant to Henry Halleck, January 18, 1863, in ibid., 231.

6. General Order No. 13, January 30, 1863, in ibid., 265n; Grant to Julia Grant, February 11, 1863, in ibid., 311; Grant to Col. William S. Hillyer, February 27, 1863, in ibid., 368; Grant to Julia Grant, March 27, 1863, in ibid., 479–80; Grant, *Memoirs*, 1:297; S. H. Lockett, "The Defense of Vicksburg," in Johnson and Buell, eds., *Battles and Leaders*, 3:485.

7. Washburn quoted in Simpson, *Ulysses S. Grant*, 181 (Cadwallader and Elihu spelled their last names differently, with Elihu adding a final *e*); Fredriksen, ed., *American Military Leaders*, 2:609–11; Grant to Henry Halleck, April 4, 1862, in *PUSG*, 8:12.

8. Simpson, *Ulysses S. Grant*, 188; Smith, *Grant*, 236–37; David D. Porter to Grant, April 20, 1863, in *PUSG*, 8:103–4n.

9. Grant to William T. Sherman, April 24, 1863, in *PUSG*, 8:117; Grant to William T. Sherman, April 27, 1863, in ibid., 130; Grant, *Memoirs*, 1:317–18. See also Grant to Jesse Grant, April 21, 1863, in *PUSG*, 8:110.

10. Grant to David D. Porter, May 1, 1863, in *PUSG*, 8:139. See also Grant, *Memoirs*, 1:326.

11. Grant, *Memoirs*, 1:321.

12. Grant to Henry Halleck, May 3, 1863, in *PUSG*, 8:147–48; Smith, *Grant*, 238.

13. Grant, *Memoirs*, 1:328, 325. See also "Special Orders No. 110," April 20, 1863, in *PUSG*, 8:98; and Grant to Stephen A. Hurlbut, April 5, 1863, in ibid., 25.

14. William T. Sherman to John Rawlins, April 8, 1863, in *PUSG*, 8:13–14n4; Grant, *Memoirs*, 1:364–65n.

15. Grant to John C. McClernand, May 1, 1863, in *PUSG*, 8:140; John S. Bowen to Grant, May 2, 1863, in *OR*, ser. 1, 24, pt. 3:263; Grant to John S. Bowen, May 2, 1863, in *PUSG*, 8:140–41.

16. Grant to Henry Halleck, May 3, 1863, in *PUSG*, 8:147–48; Grant to David D. Porter, May 2, 1863, in ibid., 142; Grant, *Memoirs*, 1:324.

17. Charles A. Dana to Edwin M. Stanton, May 4, 1963, in *OR*, ser. 1, 24, pt. 1:84; Grant to Sherman, May 3, 1863, in *PUSG*, 8:152; William T. Sherman to [Frank P.] Blair, May 4, 1863, in *OR*, ser. 1, 24, pt. 3:271; Grant

to Sherman, May 9, 1863, in *PUSG*, 8:183; Grant to Col. William S. Hillyer, May 5, 1863, in ibid., 162; General Order No. 32, May 7, 1863, in ibid., 170–71. For additional examples of Grant's concerns with supply, see Grant to Henry Halleck, May 6, 1863, in ibid., 169; and Grant to Col. Hillyer, May 9, 1863, in ibid., 187.

18. Grant to Stephen Hurlbut, May 6, 1863, in *PUSG*, 8:170; John A. McClernand to A. J. Smith, May 13, 1863, in *OR*, ser. 1, 24, pt. 3:306; Grant, *Memoirs*, 1:332.

19. Ballard, *Vicksburg*, 261–71.

20. Grant to John McClernand, May 12, 1863, in *PUSG*, 8:204–5; Grant to Sherman, May 12, 1863, in ibid., 207; Grant to McPherson, May 14, 1863, in ibid., 217; Grant to McClernand, May 14, 1863, in *OR*, ser. 1, 24, pt. 3:310; Grant to Frank P. Blair, May 14, 1863, in *PUSG*, 8:213–14; Ballard, *Vicksburg*, 271–81.

21. Grant to Francis P. Blair, May 16, 1863, in *PUSG*, 8:222–23; Cadwallader, *Three Years with Grant*, 79; Grant, *Memoirs*, 1:342; Ballard, *Vicksburg*, 282–309.

22. Grant, *Memoirs*, 1:346, 349; Grant to Francis P. Blair, May 16, 1863, in *PUSG*, 8:222; Grant to Sherman, May 16, 1863, in ibid., 228; Grant to Sherman, May 17, 1863, in ibid., 231; Sherman to Grant, May 17, 1863, in ibid., 232n; Grant to Sherman, May 17, 1863, in ibid., 232.

23. Grant to John McClernand, May 18, 1863, and Grant to James McPherson, May 18, 1863, in *OR*, ser. 1, 24, pt. 3:324; Ballard, *Vicksburg*, 310–18.

24. Grant, *Memoirs*, 1:350; Grant to Nathaniel Banks, May 10, 1863, in *PUSG*, 8:190; Simpson, *Ulysses S. Grant*, 202.

25. Grant to Col. J. C. Kelton, July 6, 1863, in *PUSG*, 8:501–2; Grant, *Memoirs*, 1:354; Ballard, *Vicksburg*, 328–32.

26. General Field Orders, May 21, 1863, in *PUSG*, 8:245–46; Ballard, *Vicksburg*, 337–48.

27. General Field Orders, May 21, 1863, in *PUSG*, 8:245–46; Grant, *Memoirs*, 1:355.

28. Grant, *Memoirs*, 1:103, 197, 206.

29. Ibid., 357; Grant to David D. Porter, May 23, 1863, in *OR*, ser. 1, 24, pt. 3:343; Grant to Nathaniel P. Banks, May 25, 1863, in ibid., 346.

30. Grant, *Memoirs*, 1:327, 354; Cadwallader, *Three Years with Grant*, 80, 63.

31. "Special Orders No. 140," May 25, 1863, in *PUSG*, 8:267n1; Grant to Henry Halleck, May 24, 1863, in ibid., 261.

32. Grant to Col. Amory K. Johnson, May 26, 1863, in ibid., 280; Grant to Brig. Gen. Nathan Kimball, June 3, 1863, in ibid., 308–9; Grant

to Maj. Gen. John G. Parke, June 22, 1863, in ibid., 407; Grant to Henry Halleck, May 29, 1863, in ibid., 283. See also Grant to William T. Sherman, June 25, 1863, in ibid., 423; and Grant to Lt. Col. Samuel J. Nasmith, June 25, 1863, in ibid., 426.

33. Grant to Nathaniel Banks, May 25, 1863, in ibid., 268; Grant to Nathaniel Banks, May 13, 1863, in ibid., 294–95; Grant to Nathaniel Banks, June 30, 1863, in ibid., 446–47.

34. Benjamin Prentiss to Grant, May 29, 1863, in ibid., 272–73n; Capt. Richard McAllister to Lt. Col. John A. Rawlins, June 4, 1863, in ibid., 346n3; Halleck to Grant, June 12, 1863, in ibid., 345n; Grant to Maj. Gen. Francis J. Herron, June 16, 1863, in ibid., 383.

35. Charles Dana to Edwin M. Stanton, April 27, 1863, in ibid., 254n; Henry Halleck to John McClernand, August 20, 1863, in ibid., 331n; Grant, *Memoirs*, 1:294; Edwin M. Stanton to Charles Dana, May 5, 1863, in *OR*, ser. 1, 24, pt. 1:84; William T. Sherman to John Rawlins, June 17, 1863, in *PUSG*, 8:429n; James McPherson to Grant, June 18, 1863, in ibid., 430n; Grant to Henry Halleck, June 19, 1863, in ibid., 385. See also *OR*, ser. 1, 24, pt. 1:102–3. For examples of McClernand's run-ins with Grant, see Grant to Henry Halleck, May 24, 1863, in *PUSG*, 8:261; and Grant, *Memoirs*, 1:294, 300, 342, 346–47, 355–56, 367. See also Simpson, *Ulysses S. Grant*, 205–6, 209–11; and Ballard, *Vicksburg*, 148–49, 156.

36. Grant to Julia Grant, December 13, 1862, in *PUSG*, 8:24. For an example of Rawlins's monitoring of Grant's drinking (a reference to the June 1863 incident), see John Rawlins to Grant, June 6, 1863, in *PUSG*, 8:322–23. For Simpson's analysis, see Simpson, *Ulysses S. Grant*, 206–8. Dana quoted in Waugh, *U. S. Grant*, 62–63. The newspaper reporter Sylvanus Cadwallader commented extensively on Grant's drinking in *Three Years with Grant*, 70–72, 103–11, 116. See also Smith, *Grant*, 231; and Waugh, *U. S. Grant*, 38–40.

37. John C. Pemberton, "The Terms of Surrender," in Johnson and Buel, eds., *Battles and Leaders*, 3:543; Grant to John Pemberton, July 3, 1863, in *PUSG*, 8:455; Grant, *Memoirs*, 1:375; Ballard, *Vicksburg*, 396–98.

38. Grant to Henry Halleck, July 4, 1863, in *PUSG*, 8:469; Grant to David D. Porter, July 3, 1863, in ibid., 459n. See also Pemberton, "The Terms of Surrender," in Johnson and Buel, eds., *Battles and Leaders*, 3:543.

39. Grant to William T. Sherman, July 3, 1863, in *PUSG*, 8:460; William T. Sherman to Grant, July 3, 1863, in ibid., 461n; William T. Sherman to John A. Rawlins, July 3, 1863, in ibid., 462n; William T. Sherman to Grant, July 4, 1863, in ibid., 478n; William T. Sherman to Grant, July 4, 1863, in *OR*, ser. 1, 24, pt. 3:472. See also Grant to E. O. C. Ord, July 4, 1863, in *PUSG*, 8:474; and Grant, *Memoirs*, 1:380. Sherman had issued orders on

July 3 for his troops to be ready to march "on short notice, with ten days' rations of flour and hard bread, coffee, salt, and sugar." General Order No. 50, July 3, 1863, in *OR*, ser. 1, 24, pt. 3:466.

40. Grant, *Memoirs*, 1:386; *New York World*, February 20, 1863, cited in Smith, *Grant*, 232; Grant, *Memoirs*, 1:354; Report of Henry Halleck to Edwin Stanton, November 15, 1863, in *OR*, ser. 1, 24, pt. 1:6. For an additional example of Sherman's skepticism, see Sherman, *Memoirs*, 1:343.

41. Grant, *Memoirs*, 1:305; Foote, *The Civil War*, 2:217 (first Lincoln quotation); Smith, *Grant*, 215 (second Lincoln quotation); Lincoln to Grant, July 13, 1863, in *PUSG*, 9:197n1 (third Lincoln quotation).

5. Chattanooga

1. Edwin Stanton to Grant, July 4, 1863, in *PUSG*, 9:20; Henry Halleck to Grant, July 7, 1863, in ibid., 69. See also ibid., xiii.

2. John A. Rawlins to Francis J. Herron, July 11, 1863, in ibid., 29n; Grant to William T. Sherman, July 13, 1863, in ibid., 43; William T. Sherman to Grant, July 14, 1863, in ibid., 45–46n; William T. Sherman to Grant, July 22, 1863, in ibid., 67; Grant to William T. Sherman, July 17, 1863, in ibid., 66. See also Grant to William T. Sherman, July 11, 1863, in ibid., 35.

3. Henry Halleck to Grant, July 11, 1863, ibid., 111n; Grant to Henry Halleck, July 18, 1863, in ibid., 70; William T. Sherman to Grant, July 12, 1863, in ibid., 36n; Henry Halleck to Grant, July 22, 1863, in ibid., 71; Grant, *Memoirs*, 1:388; Grant to Henry Halleck, July 24, 1863, in *PUSG*, 9:109. See also Grant to Col. John C. Kelton, September 25, 1863, in ibid., 238; and Grant to Henry Halleck, September 30, 1863, in ibid., 251.

4. Cadwallader, *Three Years with Grant*, 132–33; Fredriksen, ed., *American Military Leaders*, 2:676–78. For a discussion of the Battle of Chickamauga, see Woodworth, *Six Armies in Tennessee*, 79–128 (chaps. 4–5).

5. Woodworth, *Six Armies in Tennessee*, 129–49.

6. Henry Halleck to Grant, October 16, 1863, in *PUSG*, 9:296–97n; Henry Halleck to Grant, October 20, 1863, in ibid., 300n; Simpson, *Ulysses S. Grant*, 225–27.

7. Henry Halleck to Grant, October 16, 1863, in *PUSG*, 9:297n; Grant to George H. Thomas, October 19, 1863, and George H. Thomas to Grant, October 19, 1863, in *OR*, ser. 1, 30, pt. 4:479; John Rawlins to Mary E. Hurlbut, November 23, 1863, in *PUSG*, 9:298; Henry Halleck to Grant, October 20, 1863, in ibid., 299n; Grant, *Memoirs*, 1:409–10.

8. Fredriksen, ed., *American Military Leaders*, 2:808–10; George Thomas to Grant, October 19, 1863, in *PUSG*, 9:302n; Grant, *Memoirs*, 1:409–10.

9. Grant, *Memoirs,* 1:409–10; Grant to Ambrose Burnside, October 20, 1863, in *PUSG,* 9:305.

10. Porter, *Campaigning with Grant,* v, 3–5; Simpson, *Ulysses S. Grant,* 228–29; Smith, *Grant,* 266–67.

11. Grant to Henry Halleck, October 28, 1863, in *PUSG,* 9:335; Porter, *Campaigning with Grant,* 10. See also John Rawlins to Mary Hurlbut, October 27, 1863, in *PUSG,* 9:336; and Grant, *Memoirs,* 1:413, 418–19.

12. Henry M. Cist, "Comments on General Grant's 'Chattanooga,'" in Johnson and Buel, eds., *Battles and Leaders,* 3:718; William Farrar Smith, "Comments on General Grant's 'Chattanooga,'" in ibid., 714; Grant to Henry Halleck, October 26, 1863, in *PUSG,* 9:320; Grant, *Memoirs,* 2:414–17; John Rawlins to Mary Hurlbut, October 27, 1863, quoted in Simpson, *Ulysses S. Grant,* 231; Smith, *Grant,* 268; Woodworth, *Six Armies in Tennessee,* 155.

13. Grant to Henry Halleck, October 28, 1863, in *PUSG,* 9:335; Grant to William T. Sherman, October 24, 1863, in *OR,* ser. 1, 31, pt. 1:713; William T. Sherman to Grant, October 30, 1863, in *PUSG,* 9:315; Grant to Ambrose Burnside, November 1, 1863, in ibid., 342–43; Grant to Henry Halleck, November 2, 1863, in ibid., 349.

14. Smith, *Grant,* 271; Grant to Ambrose Burnside, November 7, 1863, in *PUSG,* 9:368–69; Grant to John B. Anderson, November 6, 1863, in ibid., 367; Grant to William T. Sherman, November 7, 1863, in ibid., 370; Grant to Henry Halleck, November 7, 1863, in *OR,* ser. 1, 31, pt. 3:74.

15. Grant to George H. Thomas, November 7, 1863, in *PUSG,* 9:371; Grant to Ambrose Burnside, November 8, 1863, in ibid., 374–75; Ambrose Burnside to Grant, November 12, 1863, in ibid., 375n; Grant to William Smith, November 12, 1863, in ibid., 386; Henry Halleck to Grant, November 16, 1863, and Grant to Henry Halleck, November 16, 1863, in ibid., 404; Grant to Ambrose Burnside, November 14, 1863, in ibid., 393; Grant to Ambrose Burnside, November 15, 1863, in ibid., 401; Grant to Julia Grant, November 14, 1863, in ibid., 396. See also Grant to Ambrose Burnside, November 17, 1863, in ibid., 405.

16. Grant to Henry Halleck, November 21, 1863, in ibid., 428; Grant to Charles R. Woods, November 22, 1863, in ibid., 433; William T. Sherman to Grant, November 23, 1863, in ibid., 431; Simpson, *Ulysses S. Grant,* 237–44; Smith, *Grant,* 273–75.

17. Grant to Henry Halleck, October 26, 1863, in *PUSG,* 9:321; Simpson, *Ulysses S. Grant,* 237–44; Smith, *Grant,* 275–76.

18. Grant to Elihu Washburne, December 2, 1863, in *PUSG,* 9:491; Grant, *Memoirs,* 2:445; Joseph S. Fullerton, "The Army of the Cumberland

at Chattanooga," in Johnson and Buel, eds., *Battles and Leaders*, 3:725; Simpson, *Ulysses S. Grant*, 239–44; Woodworth, *Six Armies in Tennessee*, 241–42, 195–202; Smith, *Grant*, 282–83. See also Cadwallader, *Three Years with Grant*, 151.

19. Grant to William T. Sherman, November 25, 1863, in *PUSG*, 9:447n; John A. Rawlins to George Thomas, November 25, 1863, in ibid., 448n; Grant to William T. Sherman, November 25, 1863, in ibid., 452; Grant to Henry Halleck, November 28, 1863, in ibid., 459.

20. Grant to William T. Sherman, November 25, 1863, in ibid., 451; Grant to Henry Halleck, November 27, 1863, in ibid., 455–56; Grant to Gordon Granger, November 29, 1863, in ibid., 467; Grant, *Memoirs*, 2:448, 453–55; Grant to William T. Sherman, November 29, 1863, in *PUSG*, 9:473–74; Grant to John G. Foster, November 29, 1863, in ibid., 459; Grant to Ambrose Burnside, November 29, 1863, in ibid., 465. See also Grant to Ambrose Burnside, November 29, 1863, in *OR*, ser. 1, 31, pt. 3:273; Simpson, *Ulysses S. Grant*, 242–44; and Woodworth, *Six Armies in Tennessee*, 203–5.

21. Grant to James McPherson, December 1, 1863, in *PUSG*, 9:480; Grant to Henry Halleck, December 7, 1863, in ibid., 500–501; Robert E. Lee to Jefferson Davis, December 3, 1863, in *OR*, ser. 1, 31, pt. 3:780; P. G. T. Beauregard to Pierre Soulé, December 8, 1863, in ibid., 814; Grant to John G. Foster, December 6, 1863, in *PUSG*, 9:496–98; Smith, *Grant*, 282–83. See also Grant to William T. Sherman, December 1, 1863, in *PUSG*, 9:481–82; and Grant, *Memoirs*, 2:466.

22. Woodworth, *Six Armies in Tennessee*, 195.

23. Abraham Lincoln to Grant, December 8, 1863, in Basler et al., eds., *The Collected Works of Abraham Lincoln*, 7:53; Grant, *Memoirs*, 2:450.

24. O. O. Howard to Senator Henry Wilson, December 27, 1863, quoted in Catton, *Grant Takes Command*, 55–56; Col. L. B. Eaton quoted in ibid., 56; Cadwallader, *Three Years with Grant*, 152; William T. Sherman to Grant, December 29, 1863, in *PUSG*, 9:555n2.

25. Cadwallader, *Three Years with Grant*, 154.

26. Joseph Hooker to Edwin Stanton, February 25, 1864, in *PUSG*, 9:461–62n1; Grant to John C. Kelton, December 23, 1863, in ibid., 564; Henry Halleck to Grant, November 23, 1863, in ibid., 440n; Abraham Lincoln to Grant, November 25, 1863, in ibid., 440n; Woodworth, *Six Armies in Tennessee*, 203–5.

27. Adams quoted in Williams, *McClellan, Sherman, and Grant*, 83; Charles A. Dana to Elihu Washburne, August 29, 1863, in *PUSG*, 9:219n; David Hunter to Edwin Stanton, December 14, 1863, in ibid., 476n; John A. Rawlins to Mary E. Hurlbut, October 20, 1863, in ibid., 304n.

6. The Overland Campaign

1. Grant to George Thomas, January 19, 1864, in *PUSG,* 10:46; Grant to John M. Schofield, February 11, 1864, in ibid., 102; Grant to Alvin P. Hovey, February 9, 1864, in ibid., 97.

2. James H. Wilson to Grant, February 8, 1864, in *PUSG,* 10:39n; Lincoln quoted in Catton, *Grant Takes Command,* 120.

3. For Lincoln's speech on March 9, 1864, see *PUSG,* 10:195n.

4. Porter, *Campaigning with Grant,* 26. See also Grant, *Memoirs,* 2:473.

5. Stoddard, *Lincoln's Third Secretary,* 197–98; Porter, *Campaigning with Grant,* 22.

6. William Sherman to Grant, March 10, 1864, in *PUSG,* 10:187n.

7. Grant, *Memoirs,* 2:469–70; Porter, *Campaigning with Grant,* 31.

8. Porter, *Campaigning with Grant,* 25; Grant to Charles A. Dana, August 5, 1863, in *PUSG,* 10:146–47; Smith, *Grant,* 291.

9. Lincoln quoted in McPherson, *Battle Cry of Freedom,* 667; Grant, *Memoirs,* 2:471; Smith, *Grant,* 293.

10. Grant to Brig. Gen. John E. Smith, April 26, 1864, in *PUSG,* 10:357; Wainwright, Meade's staff officer, the Wisconsin veteran, and the Second Corps officer quoted in Catton, *Grant Takes Command,* 155, 159–60; New England soldier quoted in Smith, *Grant,* 306.

11. Grant to Henry Halleck, January 15, 1864, in *PUSG,* 10:39–40; Abraham Lincoln to Don Carlos Buell, January 13, 1862, in Basler et al., eds., *The Collected Works of Abraham Lincoln,* 5:98; Grant, *Memoirs,* 2:477, 486; Catton, *Grant Takes Command,* 168. See also Grant's report to Edwin M. Stanton, July 22, 1864, in *OR,* ser. 1, 36, pt. 1:12.

12. Grant to Henry Halleck, March 24, 1864, in *PUSG,* 10:218; Grant to William T. Sherman, April 9, 1864, in ibid., 277–78; Grant and Stanton exchange quoted in Smith, *Grant,* 297.

13. For examples of Grant's campaign orders, see Grant to Nathaniel Banks, March 15, 31, April 17, 1864, in *PUSG,* 10:200–201, 243, 299; and Grant to Benjamin Butler, April 2, 16, 1864, in ibid., 245–46, 293.

14. Grant to William Sherman, April 4, 1864, in ibid., 252; William Sherman to Cyrus B. Comstock, April 5, 1864, in ibid., 219n; Sherman, *Memoirs,* 2:491.

15. Henry Halleck to Grant, February 17, 1864, in *PUSG,* 10:110n; Grant to George Meade, April 9, 1864, in ibid., 274. See also Grant, *Memoirs,* 2:482n.

16. Badeau quoted in Catton, *Grant Takes Command,* 134; Grant to Abraham Lincoln, May 1, 1864, in *PUSG,* 10:380. See also Porter, *Campaigning with Grant,* 38; and Smith, *Grant,* 310–11.

17. Grant to Julia Grant, May 2, 1864, in *PUSG,* 10:394; Porter, *Campaigning with Grant,* 37–38; Grant to William Sherman, May 2, 1864, in *PUSG,* 10:355n. See also Grant to Benjamin Butler, April 28, May 2, 1864, in ibid., 364, 366n.

18. Grant to Henry Halleck, May 4, 1864, in *OR,* ser. 1, 36, pt. 1:1; Grant to George Meade, May 5, 1864, in *PUSG,* 10, 399; Grant, *Memoirs,* 2:527.

19. Smith, *Grant,* 320–24; Porter, *Campaigning with Grant,* 54; William R. Rowley to George Meade, May 5, 1864, in *PUSG,* 10:400n; Catton, *Grant Takes Command,* 194.

20. Porter, *Campaigning with Grant,* 59–60.

21. Ibid., 69–70; Smith, *Grant,* 329–33.

22. Lincoln quoted in Smith, *Grant,* 284; Wing quoted in ibid., 334.

23. Grant to George Meade, May 7, 1864, in *PUSG,* 10:408; Grant to Henry Halleck, May 8, 1864, in *OR,* ser. 1, 36, pt. 1:2; Foote, *The Civil War,* 3:191, 132; Allen, *Down in Dixie,* 188; Rhodes, *All for the Union,* 146; Porter, *Campaigning with Grant,* 79. See also Grant, *Memoirs,* 2:539; Smith, *Grant,* 38; Catton, *Grant Takes Command,* 208–9; and Simpson, *Ulysses S. Grant,* 300–301.

24. Porter, *Campaigning with Grant,* 65, 47; Cadwallader, *Three Years with Grant,* 182; Longstreet quoted in Porter, *Campaigning with Grant,* 47; William T. Sherman, "The Grand Strategy of the Last Year of the War," in Johnson and Buel, eds., *Battles and Leaders,* 4:248.

25. Porter, *Campaigning with Grant,* 66.

26. Ibid., 86–91; Grant to Henry Halleck, May 10, 1864, in *OR,* ser. 1, 36, pt. 1:3; Grant's frustration quoted in Coffin, *Redeeming the Republic,* 112. See also Smith, *Grant,* 346–47; and Simpson, *Ulysses S. Grant,* 305–7.

27. Grant to Edwin M. Stanton, May 11, 1864, in *PUSG,* 10:422; Grant, *Memoirs,* 2:552–53n.

28. Porter, *Campaigning with Grant,* 102, 105, 108; Grant to Ambrose Burnside, May 12, 1864, in *PUSG,* 10:432; George Meade to Grant, May 12, 1864, and Grant to George Meade, May 12, 1864, in ibid., 433; Grant, *Memoirs,* 2:554; Louisiana and North Carolina soldiers quoted in Catton, *Grant Takes Command,* 235–36.

29. Porter, *Campaigning with Grant,* 113–14; Grant, *Memoirs,* 2:556n; Grant to George Meade, May 13, 1864, in *PUSG,* 10:441.

30. Grant to Julia Grant, May 13, 1864, in *PUSG,* 10:444.

31. Grant to Henry Halleck, May 16, 1864, in *OR,* ser. 1, 36, pt. 1:5; Porter, *Campaigning with Grant,* 124–25; Grant, *Memoirs,* 2:558; Grant to George Meade, May 18, 1864, in *PUSG,* 10:464. See also Grant to Henry Halleck, May 16, 1864, in ibid., 452; Grant to Henry Halleck, May 17,

1864, in ibid., 459–60; Grant, *Memoirs,* 2:557–58n, 560; and Porter, *Campaigning with Grant,* 121.

32. Grant to George Meade, May 25, 1864, in *PUSG,* 10:489; Grant to Henry Halleck, May 26, 1864, in ibid., 490; Porter, *Campaigning with Grant,* 153–54; Charles A. Dana to Edwin M. Stanton, May 26, 1864, in *OR,* ser. 1, 36, pt. 1:79; Grant to Henry Halleck, May 26, 1863, in ibid., 9; Lincoln quoted in Waugh, *U. S. Grant,* 86. See also Grant, *Memoirs,* 2:568–69.

33. Charles A. Dana to Edwin M. Stanton, May 30, 1864, in *OR,* ser. 1, 36, pt. 1:82; Grant, *Memoirs,* 2:580–83; Grant to George Meade, June 2, 1864, in *PUSG,* 11:8; Smith, *Grant,* 361.

34. Grant to George Meade, June 3, 1864, in *PUSG,* 11:14n; Grant to George Meade, June 3, 1864, in ibid., 13; Grant, *Memoirs,* 2:584; Porter, *Campaigning with Grant,* 176–78.

35. Porter, *Campaigning with Grant,* 179; Grant, *Memoirs,* 2:588.

36. Badeau, *Military History of Ulysses S. Grant,* 2:317–18; James Keleher, Third New York Regiment, June 8, 1864, quoted in Smith, *Grant,* 366; Meade, *Life and Letters,* 2:196.

37. Cadwallader, *Three Years with Grant,* 214–15.

7. Richmond, Petersburg, and Peace

1. Grant to Henry Halleck, June 5, 1864, in Grant, *Memoirs,* 2:591n.

2. Porter, *Campaigning with Grant,* 197–98; soldier quoted in Simpson, *Ulysses S. Grant,* 344; Lincoln quoted in Smith, *Grant,* 372; Catton, *Grant Takes Command,* 281–83.

3. Catton, *Grant Takes Command,* 288–89; Simpson, *Ulysses S. Grant,* 337.

4. Porter, *Campaigning with Grant,* 205–6; Grant to George Meade, June 18, 1864, in *PUSG,* 11:78; Simpson, *Ulysses S. Grant,* 337–39; Catton, *Grant Takes Command,* 290–95.

5. Smith, *Grant,* 375–76; Hankinson, *Vicksburg, 1863,* 86; Grant, *Memoirs,* 2:599.

6. Adams quoted in Simpson, *Ulysses S. Grant,* 341; Adm. Samuel P. Lee quoted in Porter, *Campaigning with Grant,* 223; Sherman quoted in ibid., 290–91; Lincoln quoted in Catton, *Grant Takes Command,* 295; Grant quoted in Foote, *Civil War,* 3:443; Wells, *Diary,* 2:58; Smith, *Grant,* 337.

7. Grant, *Memoirs,* 2:620; Porter, *Campaigning with Grant,* 278.

8. Porter, *Campaigning with Grant,* 238–40; Simpson, *Ulysses S. Grant,* 355–57; Smith, *Grant,* 377–78; McPherson, *Battle Cry of Freedom,* 756–58.

9. Sears, *Gettysburg,* 52; Grant to Henry Halleck, August 1, 1864, in

PUSG, 11:358; Abraham Lincoln to Grant, August 3, 1864, in ibid., 360n; Grant to Henry Halleck, July 14, 1864, in ibid., 242–43; Grant to Philip Sheridan, August 7, 1864, in ibid., 380; Grant to Philip Sheridan, August 26, 1864, in ibid., 12:97; Grant, *Memoirs*, 2:614–21, 627–28, 803–4; Porter, *Campaigning with Grant*, 236; Smith, *Grant*, 379–80, 384–86; Simpson, *Ulysses S. Grant*, 367–69, 378–80.

10. Henry Halleck to Grant, August 11, 1864, in *PUSG*, 11:425n; Grant to Henry Halleck, August 15, 1864, in ibid., 424; Abraham Lincoln to Grant, August 17, 1864, in ibid., 425n; Grant to Elihu Washburne, August 16, 1864, in ibid., 12:16–17; Porter, *Campaigning with Grant*, 279; Smith, *Grant*, 381–82; Simpson, *Ulysses S. Grant*, 372.

11. Grant, *Memoirs*, 2:655; Edwin Stanton to Grant, December 2, 1864, in *PUSG*, 13:50n. As early as October 29, 1864, Grant sent his aide John Rawlins to St. Louis to expedite the movement of reinforcements to Thomas's command. See Porter, *Campaigning with Grant*, 318.

12. Grant to George Thomas, December 2, 5, 6, 8, 1864, in *PUSG*, 13:53, 67, 77, 87–77; Grant to Henry Halleck, December 8, 1864, in ibid., 83; Henry Halleck to Grant, December 8, 1864, in ibid., 84n; Grant to George Thomas, December 11, 1864, in ibid., 107; George Thomas to Grant, December 11, 1864, in ibid., 107n; Special Orders No. 149, December 13, 1864, in ibid., 128n; Grant to George Thomas, December 15, 1864, in ibid., 124; Simpson, *Ulysses S. Grant*, 393–99; Smith, *Grant*, 389–90.

13. Porter, *Campaigning with Grant*, 347.

14. Sherman quoted in Foote, *The Civil War*, 3:13; Millett and Maslowski, *For the Common Defense*, 232–34; William Sherman to Grant, August 19, 1864, in *PUSG*, 12:34n; Simpson, *Ulysses S. Grant*, 347–48, 377, 389.

15. Grant to Jesse Grant, September 5, 1864, in *PUSG*, 12:130; Grant to Elihu Washburne, August 16, 1864, in ibid., 16; Simpson, *Ulysses S. Grant*, 377; Smith, *Grant*, 382.

16. Grant to William Sherman, September 10, 1864, in *PUSG*, 12:144; William Sherman to Grant, October 1, 1864, in ibid., 274n; Grant to William Sherman, November 1, 1864, in ibid., 370–71; William Sherman to Grant, November 2, 1864, in ibid., 371n; Grant to William Sherman, November 2, 1864, in *PUSG*, 12:373; *New York Times* reporter quoted in Simpson, *Ulysses S. Grant*, 391; Lincoln quoted in Sandburg, *Abraham Lincoln*, 339; Simpson, *Ulysses S. Grant*, 382–84, 390–91; Smith, *Grant*, 388–89.

17. Grant to George Meade, July 24, 1864, in *PUSG*, 11:306; Grant to George Meade, July 28, 1864, in ibid., 333; Grant, *Memoirs*, 2:608; Simpson, *Ulysses S. Grant*, 361; Catton, *Grant Takes Command*, 319.

18. Grant to Henry Halleck, August 1, 1864, in *PUSG*, 11:361; testimony before the Committee on the Conduct of the War quoted in Catton,

Grant Takes Command, 325; Simpson, *Ulysses S. Grant,* 360–67; Catton, *Grant Takes Command,* 320–25.

19. Porter, *Campaigning with Grant,* 310–11; Grant, *Memoirs,* 2:630; Simpson, *Ulysses S. Grant,* 386–87.

20. Porter, *Campaigning with Grant,* 372–73.

21. Grant to Edwin Stanton, February 4, 1865, in *PUSG,* 13:362.

22. Robert E. Lee to Grant, March 2, 1865, in ibid., 14:99n; Grant to Edwin Stanton, March 3, 1865, in ibid., 90; Edwin Stanton to Grant, March 3, 1865, in ibid., 91n; Grant to Edwin Stanton, March 4, 1865, in ibid., 100; Grant to Robert E. Lee, March 4, 1865, in ibid., 98; Porter, *Campaigning with Grant,* 390.

23. Grant to George Meade, March 14, 1865, in *PUSG,* 14:160; Grant to George Meade, March 14, 1865, in ibid., 159; Grant, *Memoirs,* 2:687–88, 691.

24. Simpson, *Ulysses S. Grant,* 418; Catton, *Grant Takes Command,* 437–39; Smith, *Grant,* 393–94; Cadwallader, *Three Years with Grant,* 297–98.

25. George Meade to Grant, March 21, 22, 1865, in *PUSG,* 14:214n; Grant to George Meade, March 24, 1865, in ibid., 211–14; Grant to Philip Sheridan, March 28, 1865, in ibid., 243.

26. Grant to Philip Sheridan, March 29, 1865, in ibid., 253; Porter, *Campaigning with Grant,* 427–29.

27. Grant to Meade, April 1, 1865, in *PUSG,* 14:297–98; Porter, *Campaigning with Grant,* 430, 444; Grant, *Memoirs,* 2:708; George Meade (Wright) to Grant, April 1, 1865, in *PUSG,* 14:300n; Grant to Edward Ord, April 1, 1865, in ibid., 302–3.

28. Lee quoted in Smith, *Grant,* 394–95; Porter, *Campaigning with Grant,* 447; Grant to Philip Sheridan, April 2, 1865, in *PUSG,* 14:320.

29. Grant to George Meade, April 3, 1865, in *PUSG,* 14:334n; Grant to Edward Ord, April 3, 1865, in ibid., 335; Grant to Philip Sheridan, April 3, 1865, in ibid., 366; Grant to William Sherman, April 3, 1865, in ibid., 338–39; Porter, *Campaigning with Grant,* 448–49.

30. Grant to George Meade, April 4, 1865, in *PUSG,* 14:343; Grant to Philip Sheridan, April 4, 1865, in ibid., 344; Grant, *Memoirs,* 2:714; Porter, *Campaigning with Grant,* 453.

31. Philip Sheridan to Grant, April 5, 1865, in *PUSG,* 14:348n; Grant to George Meade, April 5, 1865, in ibid., 350; Grant to William Sherman, April 5, 1865, in ibid., 352; soldier quoted in Porter, *Campaigning with Grant,* 456; Grant to Theodore S. Bowers, April 6, 1865, in *PUSG,* 14:360; Sherman, *Memoirs,* 2:831; Cadwallader, *Three Years with Grant,* 313.

32. Philip Sheridan to Grant, April 6, 1865, and Abraham Lincoln to Grant, April 6, 1865, in *PUSG,* 14:358n; Grant to William Sherman, April

6, 1864, in ibid., 14:359; Grant to Robert E. Lee, April 7, 1865, in ibid., 361; Longstreet quoted in Smith, *Grant*, 400. For the exchange of messages between Grant and Lee, see *PUSG*, 14:361, 367, 371. Grant to Philip Sheridan, April 8, 1865, in ibid., 369; Grant to Edwin Stanton, April 9, 1865, in ibid., 371.

33. Grant to Robert E. Lee, April 9, 1865, in *PUSG*, 14:373–74; Grant to Edwin Stanton, April 9, 1865, in ibid., 375n; Simpson, *Ulysses S. Grant*, 429–36; Smith, *Grant*, 399–407.

34. Grant, *Memoirs*, 2:735, 741; Porter, *Campaigning with Grant*, 486, 514; Cadwallader, *Three Years with Grant*, 288–89; Smith, *Grant*, 404.

35. Grant to John Pope, April 16, 1865, in *PUSG*, 14:394; Grant to Edward Canby, April 17, 1865, in ibid., 398; Grant to Philip Sheridan, April 15, 16, in ibid., 393, 395; William Sherman to Grant, April 18, 1865, in ibid., 419–20n; Simpson, *Ulysses S. Grant*, 444–48.

36. Smith, *Grant*, 410.

37. Grant to Charles W. Ford, April 17, 1865, in *PUSG*, 14:405; Maj. Thomas T. Eckert to Grant, April 15, 1865, in ibid., 390n; Grant quoted in Smith, *Grant*, 409–11; Simpson, *Ulysses S. Grant*, 442–44. See also Grant to Julia Grant, April 20, 1865, in *PUSG*, 14:422.

8. A Faith in Success

1. Stanton quoted in Donald, *Lincoln*, 599; Smith, *Grant*, 294.

2. Lincoln quoted in Williams, *Lincoln and His Generals*, 21; McPherson, *Battle Cry of Freedom*, 396–402.

3. There is some dispute over whether Hooker actually made such a confession after Chancellorsville. See Sears, *Chancellorsville*, 504–5.

4. Mary Lincoln quoted in Keckley, *Behind the Scenes*, 45–46.

5. Bonekemper, *A Victor, Not a Butcher*, 266–68, 323. See also Fuller, *The Generalship of Ulysses S. Grant*, 371–72.

6. Grant, *Memoirs*, 2:485; Grant to Julia Grant, February 24, 1862, in *PUSG*, 4:284 (emphasis added); Porter, *Campaigning with Grant*, 1811.

7. Grant, *Memoirs*, 2:485; Charles A. Dana to Edwin M. Stanton, May 25, 1864, in *OR*, ser. 1, 36, pt. 1:78.

8. Porter, *Campaigning with Grant*, 64–64, 103, 164. See also ibid., 123, 183; Grant, *Memoirs*, 1:119; and Simpson, *Ulysses S. Grant*, 45.

9. Sherman, *Memoirs*, 1:428; Porter, *Campaigning with Grant*, 515; Ingalls and aide quoted in ibid., 340; Cadwallader, *Three Years with Grant*, 352–53; Grant, *Memoirs*, 1:73.

10. Buckner quoted in Porter, *Campaigning with Grant*, 382; Simpson, *Ulysses S. Grant*, 24 (first Longstreet quotation); Porter, *Campaigning with*

Grant, 515–16 (second Longstreet quotation); Smith, *Grant,* 92–93. See also Porter, *Campaigning with Grant,* 328, 341–42, 356–57, 395.

11. Grant to Julia Grant, December 24, 1864, in *PUSG,* 13:163; William Sherman to Grant, March 4, 1864, in Sherman, *Memoirs,* 1:428.

12. Clausewitz, *On War,* 145; Porter, *Campaigning with Grant,* 248–49.

13. Sherman quoted in Catton, *Grant Takes Command,* 160.

Bibliography

Primary Sources

Allen, Stanton P. *Down in Dixie: Life in a Cavalry Regiment in the War Days, from the Wilderness to Appomattox.* Boston: D. Lothrop, 1892.

Badeau, Adam. *Military History of Ulysses S. Grant.* New York: D. Appleton, 1868–1881.

Basler, Roy P., et al., eds. *The Collected Works of Abraham Lincoln.* 8 vols. New Brunswick, NJ: Rutgers University Press, 1953–1955.

Brinton, John H. *Personal Memoirs of John H. Brinton: Civil War Surgeon, 1861–1865.* Carbondale: Southern Illinois University Press, 1996.

Cadwallader, Sylvanus. *Three Years with Grant.* Lincoln: University of Nebraska Press, 1996.

Clausewitz, Carl von. *On War.* New York: Penguin, 1968.

Grant, Ulysses S. *Personal Memoirs of U. S. Grant.* In *Memoirs and Selected Letters* (2 vols. in 1, continuously paginated). New York: Literary Classics of the United States, 1990.

Johnson, Robert U., and Clarence C. Buel, eds. *Battles and Leaders of the Civil War.* 4 vols. New York: Century, 1887.

Keckley, Elizabeth. *Behind the Scenes; or, Thirty Years a Slave, and Four Years in the White House.* Teddington: Echo, 2008.

Meade, George. *The Life and Letters of George Gordon Meade.* New York: Scribner's, 1913.

Porter, Horace. *Campaigning with Grant.* Lincoln: University of Nebraska Press, 2000.

Rhodes, Robert Hunt, ed. *All for the Union: The Civil War Diary and Letters of Elisha Hunt Rhodes.* New York: Orion, 1985.

Sherman, William T. *Memoirs of General W. T. Sherman.* 2 vols. in 1, continuously paginated. New York: Literary Classics of the United States, 1990.

Simon, John Y., ed. *The Papers of Ulysses S. Grant.* 31 vols. Carbondale: Southern Illinois University Press, 1972–2009.

Stoddard, William O. *Lincoln's Third Secretary: The Memoir of William O. Stoddard.* New York: Exposition, 1955.

Wallace, Lew. *An Autobiography.* 2 vols. New York: Harper & Bros., 1906.

War of the Rebellion: A Compilation of the Official Records of the Union and Confederate Armies. 128 vols. Washington, DC, 1880–1901.

Wells, Gideon. *Diary of Gideon Wells.* 2 vols. New York: Norton, 1960.

Secondary Sources

Ballard, Michael B. *U. S. Grant: The Making of a General, 1861–1863.* Lanham, MD: Rowman & Littlefield, 2005.

———. *Vicksburg: The Campaign That Opened the Mississippi.* Chapel Hill: University of North Carolina Press, 2004.

Bauer, K. Jack. *Zachary Taylor: Soldier, Planter, Statesman of the Old Southwest.* Baton Rouge: Louisiana State University Press, 1993.

Bonekemper, Edward H., III. *A Victor, Not a Butcher: Ulysses S. Grant's Overlooked Military Genius.* Washington, DC: Regnery, 2004.

Branson, Richard. *Losing My Virginity: How I Survived, Had Fun, and Made a Fortune Doing Business My Way.* New York: Crown, 2011.

Catton, Bruce. *Grant Moves South, 1861–1863.* New York: Little, Brown, 1960; reprint, Edison, NJ: Castle, 2000.

———. *Grant Takes Command, 1863–1865.* New York: Little, Brown, 1968; reprint, Edison, NJ: Castle, 2000.

Coffin, Charles Carleton. *Redeeming the Republic: The Third Period of the War of the Rebellion in the Year 1864.* New York: Harper Bros., 1889.

Cunningham, O. Edward. *Shiloh and the Western Campaign of 1862.* Edited by Gary D. Joiner and Timothy B. Smith. New York: Savas Beatie, 2007.

Daniel, Larry J. *Shiloh: The Battle That Changed the Civil War.* New York: Simon & Schuster, 1997.

Donald, David Herbert. *Lincoln.* New York: Simon & Schuster, 1995.

Foote, Shelby. *The Civil War: A Narrative.* 3 vols. New York: Random House, 1963–1974.

Fredriksen, John C., ed. *American Military Leaders: From Colonial Times to the Present.* 2 vols. Santa Barbara, CA: ABC-CLIO, 1999.

Fuller, J. F. C. *The Generalship of Ulysses S. Grant.* London: John Murray, 1929; reprint, Cambridge, MA: DaCapo, 1991.

Grimsley, Mark, and Steven E. Woodworth. *Shiloh: A Battlefield Guide.* Lincoln, NE: Bison, 2006.

Hankinson, Alan. *Vicksburg, 1863.* Oxford: Osprey, 1993.

Hughes, Nathaniel Cheairs, Jr. *The Battle of Belmont: Grant Strikes South.* Chapel Hill: University of North Carolina Press, 1991.

Isaacson, Walter. *Steve Jobs.* New York: Simon & Schuster, 2011.

Luvaas, Jay, Stephen Bowman, and Leonard Fullenkamp, eds. *Guide to the Battle of Shiloh.* Lawrence: University Press of Kansas, 1996.

McFeely, William S. *Grant: A Biography.* New York: Norton, 1981.

McPherson, James. *Battle Cry of Freedom: The Civil War Era*. New York: Oxford University Press, 1988.

———. *Tried by War: Abraham Lincoln as Commander in Chief*. New York: Penguin, 2008.

Millett, Allan R., and Peter Maslowski. *For the Common Defense: A Military History of the United States of America*. New York: Free Press, 1984.

Rafuse, Ethan S. "Still a Mystery? General Grant and the Historians, 1981–2006." *Journal of Military History* 71, no. 3 (July 2007): 849–74.

Reed, George, Craig Bullis, Ruth Collins, and Christopher Paprone. "Mapping the Route of Leadership Education: Caution Ahead." *Parameters* 34, no. 4 (Autumn 2004): 46–60.

Robertson, Glenn William. *The Staff Ride*. Washington, DC: Center of Military History, 1987.

Sandburg, Carl. *Abraham Lincoln: The Prairie Years and the War Years* (1954). Edited by Edward C. Goodman. New York: Sterling, 2007.

Schultz, Howard, and Joanne Gordon. *Onward: How Starbucks Fought for Its Life without Losing Its Soul*. New York: Rodale, 2011.

Sears, Stephen W. *Chancellorsville*. Boston: Houghton Mifflin, 1996.

———. *Gettysburg*. Boston: Houghton Mifflin, 2003.

Simpson, Brooks D. *Ulysses S. Grant: Triumph over Adversity, 1822–1865*. New York: Houghton Mifflin, 2000.

Smith, Jean Edward. *Grant*. New York: Simon & Schuster, 2001.

Sword, Wiley. *Shiloh: Bloody April*. Dayton, OH: Morningside, 1974.

Tsouras, Peter G., ed. *The Book of Military Quotations*. St. Paul, MN: Zenith, 1992.

Waugh, Joan. *U. S. Grant: American Hero, American Myth*. Chapel Hill: University of North Carolina Press, 2009.

Williams, T. Harry. *Lincoln and His Generals*. New York: Knopf, 1952.

———. *McClellan, Sherman, and Grant*. New Brunswick, NJ: Rutgers University Press, 1962.

Winschel, Terrence. *Vicksburg: Fall of the Confederate Gibraltar*. Abilene, TX: McWhiney Foundation Press, 1999.

Wong, Leonard, Paul Bliese, and Dennis McGurk. "Military Leadership: A Context Specific Review." *Leadership Quarterly* 14 (December 2003): 657–92.

Woodworth, Steven E. *Six Armies in Tennessee: The Chickamauga and Chattanooga Campaigns*. Lincoln: University of Nebraska Press, 1998.

Index

Wilson, James H., 106
Wing, Henry, 118
Wood, Thomas, 95

Wright, Horatio G., 121, 125–26,
134, 148

Yates, Richard, 21